My Dog Has Fallen and He Can't Get Up!

Rehabilitation from
a spinal injury with paralysis

Judy Wolff

JFTM, LLC.
Acton, Massachusetts, USA
www.jftm.biz

Printed in the United States of America.

Front cover illustration: Elish Flynn

Back cover photo: Samuels Studios, Inc. Used with permission.

All service marks, trademarks, and product names referred to herein are the property of their respective holders.

ISBN: 978-0-9827594-0-0

Library of Congress Control Number: 2010906362

Author: Wolff, Judith A.

1. Dogs—Diseases   2. Human-Animal Relationships

This book is available at quantity discounts. For information, email pubs-sales@jftm.biz.

Preface

I wrote this book as encouragement for anybody whose dog has had a fibrocartilaginous embolism. I hope that by sharing our experiences and some tips for coping with the day-to-day logistical challenges, that others might be heartened to give their dogs a chance to rehabilitate if the medical prognosis is good.

This is Tucker's story.

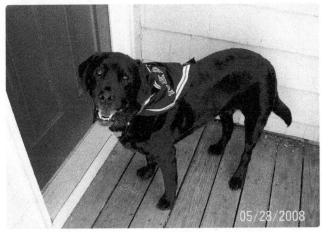

Photo: Judy Wolff

**Tucker, four days before being stricken by
a fibrocartilaginous embolism**

Introducing Tucker

We adopted Tucker, a purebred black Labrador Retriever, on January 31, 2003 from Labrador Retriever Rescue, Inc., the same organization that had given us our first dog, Sheena, seven years earlier.

(Disclosure: After several years as a volunteer, in 2008 I was elected the organization's president—also a volunteer position—for a term that I am currently serving.)

A second dog, I thought, would invigorate Sheena, who was thirteen and starting to slow down. I anticipated the day Sheena wouldn't be able to climb upstairs and might welcome a sleeping buddy downstairs.

Little did I know that I would never have been able to leave Tucker downstairs without parental supervision. While Sheena was totally trustworthy in the house, Tucker was another story altogether.

Tucker was surrendered to Labrador Retriever Rescue because his owner's work demands and weekend outings left him little time for a dog. Lack of time by the human is the most common reason dogs end up in rescue.

At the time, Tucker was three-and-a-half years old and a bit neurotic. He had some basic obedience training, including sit, down, and a fabulously reliable response to "come." Unfortunately, he also had some undesirable habits.

The first of these "issues" we witnessed was resource guarding. If he got hold of something, it was his. He did not understand the concept of "trade."

His favorite items to grab? Paper. Perfect for a house populated by avid readers who own thousands of books and have dozens of magazines coming into the house each month.

We also discovered Tucker's pathological urge to eat anything. Anything. His urges far exceed what is normal for a Lab, a breed notorious for voracious appetites. A veterinarian diagnosed him with Pica, the same disorder that compels some people to eat weird stuff, such as dirt, hairballs, and paint.

Some examples of Tucker's dietary indiscretion: banana peels, gloves, sticks, asphalt "pebbles," leaves, snow by the mouthful, corncobs, a sandal, limbs from stuffed toys, plastic bags, newspapers, magazines, a cardboard six-pack carrier, thorny poison ivy vines (which I have since cut down), discarded McDonald's ketchup packets, napkins, tissues, wood chips, and a paperback edition of Shakespeare's Julius Caesar ("I came, I saw, I swallowed.") Tucker will eat pretty much anything discarded by the roadside, except he has always minded the Surgeon General's warning and steered clear of cigarette butts.

Now think what it's like to have a dog that will swallow anything that fits in his mouth, but won't relinquish it. A dog with quick reflexes, who can inhale an item in its entirety before a human even notices it.

I knew that if the challenge ever became more than I was willing to deal with that I could return Tucker to Lab Rescue, an organization that honors a lifetime take-back guarantee on all dogs they place. But I liked him, most of the time, when he wasn't acting out.

All the dog professionals (dog trainer, veterinarian, dog walker) reassured me that he was a great dog with great potential. Knowing that potential was there to be nurtured gave me the persistence to work with him.

I think Tucker was put into my life to teach me patience. Working through Tucker's issues gave me the patience I would later need for coping with the aftermath of his spinal injury.

Another of Tucker's "issues" was a fear of new things and strangers. This stress-related behavior is not unusual for a re-homed dog, especially a nervous dog living in a home with people nervous about having a nervous dog.

Tucker's fear was expressed as barking at anything new or different: a balloon on a mailbox, a duffel bag that hadn't been in the room the day before, a trash can at the end of a driveway, or a new beach ball in the yard next door.

What was puzzling, though, was that he had two diametrically opposed greetings for strangers—and I, at the other end of the leash, couldn't predict which behavior would materialize for any specific person.

Tucker would greet most people with a goofy smile and a full body wiggle. But some people, apparently at random, he would greet with lunging and barking.

I tried to discern the characteristics common to the people he barked at. We'd stand outside the grocery store, K-Mart, Dunkin' Donuts, and other businesses with heavy foot traffic. I'd pay attention to what set him off. Nothing with certainty: not age, skin color, facial hair, hair color or length, hats or caps, canes or walkers, odd walking gait, long or short jackets, and on and on. Nothing I could see.

Until one day I realized that I, belonging to a visually-oriented species, was *looking* for cues. Maybe Tucker was *smelling* triggers. "Do you have a cat?" I would ask. Some people said no, but then would add, "But I just visited my mother, who has three cats." I learned to ask, "Have you been near a cat lately?" Bingo! Strangers with cat scent! Tucker didn't bark at friends and neighbors with cats because he was acquainted with these people. It took me two years to figure that out! Now, before strangers get within Tucker's comfort zone, I can screen them and steer clear.

Little did I know how his dislike of cats would someday paralyze him.

How did we cope with this challenging dog?

We learned new management skills. No longer would we leave books, magazines, phone bills, or tissues within dog reach. We would never, ever leave food on the counter. We installed baby gates at entrances to every room with an open door. We installed baby gates at the top and bottom of the stairs. We put more baby gates in front of bookcases and blocking access to the magazine rack. We put another baby gate on the deck for occasional use. Life with Tucker means twelve baby gates in use on any given day.

I worked on training, using a combination of classical conditioning and clicker training, a scientifically proven system of marking and rewarding desired behavior that is based on operant conditioning.

We trained in group classes and private sessions, and we took advantage of every opportunity to train in daily life. Within six months of his adoption, Tucker had passed the Canine Good Citizen test.

We continued to train. I read books about training, participated in online discussions, and attended a weekend of clicker training lectures and workshops.

We took agility classes, not with the intention of competing, but as a fun activity to let Tucker practice self-control in a stimulating environment. We went places to practice skills in different settings. Training was a fabulous bonding experience for Tucker and me.

A special bond forms between a person and a Rescue dog, in part because there's always some element of mystery about the dog's past. Has he ever gone swimming in a pool? Has he ever seen a horse? Why does he hate cats—did he have a bad encounter with one? Because I couldn't ask Tucker directly (well, I could ask, but I shouldn't expect an answer), all I could do is observe.

Surprises abound: the first time I said, "Wanna race?" Tucker shot ahead. I didn't teach him that, but apparently someone did. We play the "wanna race" game every night to go upstairs; he always wins because I walk behind him. Sometimes we race inside from the backyard; he always wins because, well, he's simply faster.

It typically takes three to six months for a Rescue dog and human to bond. Tucker and I needed a few years to get in sync, but now we communicate effectively. We know each other's routines and how much we can push each other's buttons.

For example, I know that if he makes a mistake and takes something he shouldn't have, such as the TV remote or a placemat, my immediate response sets the tone for what happens next. If I yell, lunge towards him, or show any anger or panic, Tucker will react defensively and guard the object. If, instead, I say, "Thank you!" in a happy, playful voice, Tucker will drop the object and run to me for a treat (or we run together to the refrigerator to find a special yummy, like cheese, a hardboiled egg, or peanut butter).

People who have met Tucker in the last few years don't believe me when I describe how he used to act. They see the sweet, affectionate, and funny side of his personality.

Tucker is a happy dog, needy of attention (typical of a male Lab), and not immune to the goofiness of his breed. One minute he's sniffing the ground; the next, he's zooming around the yard, in a ritual often called butt-tucking.

He plays well with other dogs, except for bullies and brats, whom he will correct appropriately. He's smart and a terrific companion.

He also loves learning new tricks. Among his favorites are playing his Fisher-Price® piano, making his Staples® Easy Button^{SM} "talk," spinning in a circle, and pushing doors open or closed. He has saluted the Grand Marshal in our town's Memorial Day parade. He makes a scary face on cue, flips a large ring over his muzzle in a game he invented that I call "ring toss."

If I tell him "I have an opportunity for you," he goes to the foot of the stairs and lies down, because I am giving him an opportunity to earn a treat by waiting for me while I deal with some matter upstairs. (If he's waiting for me, he is not wandering around looking to create mischief.)

He can ride a skateboard—at least for a few steps. I'm currently teaching him to bowl.

My favorite of his tricks? When I take the bottle of ear cleaner out of the cupboard, Tucker comes over and sits, knowing that he'll get a wonderful treat after his ears are cleaned. Ditto for having his nails trimmed, for which he gets Cheerios®.

Tucker crawls on his belly to the cue "Rin Tin Tin" and has a slow, dramatic, "dying" move when prompted with a finger-gun and "Bang!"

You know that play-bow that dogs do to invite other dogs to play? The one where they lower their shoulders and stick their butts in the air? He does that on cue, too. Very cute.

He loves playing with children. One day, a volunteer for Lab Rescue came to our house to shoot some footage of Tucker for a video she was making about the organization. She brought along her two young children. We brought Tucker into the backyard, where the lighting was better for videotaping, and where she could keep an eye on her children. Tucker had never met Heather or her children before. The kids started running around, flapping arms, and screaming as youngsters do. Tucker joined in with them, running with and after them, never once jumping on them or making any physical contact. He had a huge smile on his face throughout: what a blast! You can watch this video on YouTube. (Appendix B lists URLs for videos mentioned in the text.)

A two-year-old girl named Zoey, who lives around the corner, adores Tucker. (Her generic name for dog is, in fact, "Tucker.") She sometimes "helps" me walk Tucker by holding the end of his leash. (I hold the business part of the leash attached to his collar.) When Zoey is "walking" Tucker, he adjusts his pace to her baby steps.

Tucker knows he's handsome and will sit and pose if you bring out a camera. Seriously.

His favorite activity, besides eating, is swimming, followed by fetching objects in the water. He has mastered the "please feed this starving dog" look, with big brown eyes, tilted head, and a raised paw.

Photo: Judy Wolff

Tucker the lap dog with friend, Jake

If you sit on the floor, he'll join you—in your lap. And if you let him, he will give your face, hands, and arms a thorough tongue washing.

Although I could go on and on telling stories about Tucker, I think by now you get the picture of what a terrific dog he is. But there is much more to Tucker's story. I wrote this book to tell you about a particular life-changing event. Now that you're acquainted with the hero, let's get on with the story.

Disclaimer

Any errors in the use of medical terminology or descriptions of fibrocartilaginous embolism (FCE) and physical therapy protocols are my own alone. I'm a lay person doing my best to explain subjects in which I have no professional training.

This book describes my own experiences; it is not a veterinary or physical therapy handbook.

For the sake of your pet's well-being, please follow the advice of your own veterinarian, neurologist, and canine physical therapist over anything a "simple pet owner," such as myself, has to say.

Acknowledgments

Thanks to:

Lois Andelman, Cindy Rush, and Deanna Smith for reading the first draft and for letting me bounce ideas off them throughout this project.

Michelle Borelli for her insightful editorial comments and for making Gemini Dogs a place where I feel comfortable leaving Tucker for the day.

Everyone at Massachusetts Veterinary Referral Hospital for their compassionate and professional care, especially Charlie Evans, Beth Innis, and Gena Silver.

Karen Pryor for reviewing the references to clicker training, in particular the description of how I used the clicker to stimulate Tucker's nervous system.

Everyone who assisted me during Tucker's rehabilitation.

Special thanks to Kristen Dineen Sullivan for allowing Tucker to swim in her pool.

Contents

Photo: Samuels Studio, Inc. (used with permission)

Sheena (left) and Tucker

1

THE FALL (SUNDAY)

"Something's wrong with Tucker. He fell down and he can't get up."

So went the 3:00 P.M. phone call from my husband, David, while I was at a festival with my friend, Lois.

"What happened?"

"I'm not sure. He was in the backyard. I heard a weird yelp. It didn't sound like his bark, so I went out to check. I found him lying in the yard, trying to get up. He couldn't, so I carried him inside. What should I do?"

"Is he in pain?"

"No, he doesn't seem to be. He just can't put any weight on one of his legs."

"Any blood or swelling? Any pain if you touch his leg?"

"No, and no."

"I'm on my way home. It should take me forty minutes. Call me if anything changes. Apply an icepack to his knee for fifteen minutes to prevent swelling. Even if it's useless, it's unlikely to make things worse."

On the drive, I started thinking about what could have happened to my dog. He probably sprained something. Maybe he tore his cruciate ligament (a common injury for an active dog, one that affects one million dogs a year). Cruciate injuries are especially common among Labs. My previous Lab, Sheena, tore a cruciate ligament when she was nine. Tucker was now eight and much more athletic than Sheena ever was. I've met people at the gym who have torn knee ligaments; some have said that the initial tear was painful but afterwards they felt no pain, just instability in the joint.

You will soon see why I am not licensed to practice veterinary medicine.

With the preconception in mind that Tucker had torn a cruciate ligament, I pulled into the driveway. I ran inside and found Tucker lying in the narrow enclosed breezeway that separates the house from the garage. He didn't appear to be in pain, but he clearly was unable to stand up. He looked at me, as if I had a solution. Or maybe he just wanted a cookie.

It was a Sunday. Our regular veterinary clinic was closed. I thought, do we go to the emergency veterinary clinic? What would they do? We would wait for hours while they cared for pets with life-threatening conditions. Then they would examine Tucker's vital signs and tell us to see our own veterinarian in the morning. OK, I can take his temperature, check the color of his gums, and monitor him for signs of distress, shock, or pain. The emergency clinic is open 24 hours and is less than four miles away. If his situation worsens, we can be there in ten minutes.

While waiting, I took detailed notes in an effort to be able to supply accurate information to the veterinarian, but mostly to occupy myself.

At 4:00 P.M., an hour after his fall, Tucker vomited a small amount of bile.

He was breathing normally and was alert. There was no swelling, no blood, and no pain or reaction when I manipulated his joints.

Tucker, thankfully, is a wimpy dog and not shy about exhibiting pain. You usually don't want a dog to growl at you, but if you're trying to determine if he's in pain, a growl communicates. (If another person's handling caused *you* pain, you'd growl, too.) No matter how I handled him, Tucker didn't growl or complain. He made it clear that being injured didn't ruin his appetite.

Because he had vomited, I fed him conservatively. At 4:20 P.M., an hour after his regular dinnertime, I fed him 1/4 cup of kibble. At 4:30, his temperature read 101.2°, well within normal range. At 5:30, I fed him another 1/4 cup of his kibble.

His body temperature at 5:45 remained normal, at 101°.

Since he was still holding down food with no distress, at 6:30, I fed him another 1/4 cup of kibble. He also drank some water.

He continued to be alert and quiet, and he didn't complain about having his food dish replenished multiple times.

We would have a long wait until tomorrow morning. We all settled down and thought things through.

We needed a way to get Tucker outside, for our trip to the veterinarian, whether that's today or tomorrow, and for potty breaks. He hadn't been outside for a few hours, so that was our first priority.

There are three doors from the breezeway to the outdoors, but all ultimately require maneuvering up and down three steps. Fortunately, we had a twelve-foot wheelchair ramp in the garage. We got this ramp from a friend of a friend, who had it built for her dog, who had since passed on. The ramp had helped old, arthritic Sheena in her last months. (She died seven weeks before her fifteenth birthday.) After Sheena's death, three years earlier, we stored the ramp in the garage, expecting to someday pass it on to another dog.

3

We set up the ramp at the back door, where it led to the driveway next to the front lawn. We would need to reacquaint Tucker with the ramp, as he hadn't used it in three years. But before we could get Tucker down the ramp, we had to get him across the breezeway and out the door. You can watch our pathetic attempt, using a towel for a sling, on YouTube. (See Appendix B for the URL for this video.)

We finally got him outside, down the ramp, and onto the lawn, where, eventually, he emptied his bladder. It was 7:00 P.M. When we returned inside, I recorded these notes for the veterinarian, "left hind leg drags behind; no ability to control (lift, bear weight), foot turned under."

At the time, I did not understand the significance of that foot being turned under.

On this early June evening, the weather was mild enough that Tucker and I could sleep in the breezeway. Not that I got any sleep. I was keeping an eye on Tucker, ready to take him to the emergency clinic if he showed any sign of distress.

We made it through the night without incident. Tucker shot frequent glances at the kitchen door, ready to go inside and upstairs to the dog bed we call his "big boy bed," but climbing stairs was out of the question. He snuggled in next to me, and we both tried to sleep.

My notes read:

> "Stopped food, treats, water at 7:30 P.M. Quiet all evening, all night. Trouble shifting position. Sat or lay down all night. No vocalizing (no bark, cry, whine, moan)."

That Tucker did not vocalize was worrisome because it was unusual behavior for him. Don't tell the other dogs in his playgroup, but my 75-lb muscular Lab is a crybaby and a momma's boy.

2

Tests & Diagnosis (Monday)

The morning after Tucker's fall, we struggled with another clumsy trip outside. Using the towel sling, we inched him down the ramp and onto the front lawn.

We put Tucker on a blanket. I made a trip inside to retrieve my morning coffee, the phone, and a lawn chair, and thus settled down on the front lawn, and waited until the veterinarian's office opened.

Tucker was agitated, wanting his breakfast. I anticipated that he would be sedated for x-rays, so I didn't feed him. You might be asking, how could Tucker even want to eat, with whatever was going on with him physically? Remember, he's a Lab, so he is always, always ready to eat. But mostly he rested on the blanket and sniffed the dirt, searching, unsuccessfully, for bugs, worms, or rabbit droppings to nibble.

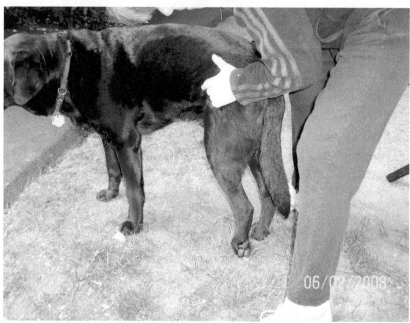

Photo: David Wolff

Helping Tucker to stand

Finally, at 8:00 A.M., I called the veterinarian's office. Answering machine. Wait another minute. Try again. Answering machine again.

I checked my watch, and called again. At last, a voice, "Village Animal Hospital [*not the real name*] How may I help you?"

"This is Judy Wolff. Tucker can't put any weight on one leg. I think he may have torn an ACL. Can someone see him this morning?"

Luckily for us, the clinic's owner, Dr. Brewer [*name changed on request*], who knew Tucker, was working that morning. She had surgery scheduled but would make time to examine him.

We lifted him onto the back seat of the car and I drove to the veterinarian's office. A veterinary technician carried him inside and into the examination room, where, as usual, he emptied his bladder from nerves. As a bonus, a brown blob of alien slime fell from his prepuce. My stomach churned. The blob turned out to be a slug from our lawn.

The look on Dr. Brewer's face when she saw Tucker churned my stomach again.

Her expression wasn't the result of seeing the slug. Although she tried to hide her concern, it was obvious that she thought Tucker's injury was much more serious than a cruciate tear.

Dr. Brewer explained that the turned-under foot, called knuckling, was symptomatic of a neurological problem, and the leg was dangling and weak not from a soft tissue injury, but from paralysis.

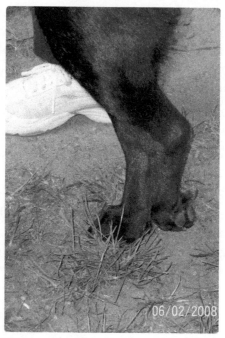

06/02/2008

Photo: David Wolff

The knuckled foot

She palpated Tucker's various joints and noted that his right hind foot responded to touch, but not his left.

Tucker was carried off into the back for x-rays, while I waited in the examination room alone. The x-rays showed no broken bones or torn ligaments.

Dr. Brewer said there were several possible causes for Tucker's paralysis: a ruptured disc, a blood clot, or a tumor in the spinal column.

She said we could treat the symptoms with intravenous steroids to reduce inflammation, but she recommended against going that route without knowing what happened to him.

She said the prognosis was, as my notes say, "~~more optimistic~~ less guarded" because he could stand on one leg. (I had crossed out "more optimistic" while scribbling my notes, as Dr. Brewer amended her wording.)

Dr. Brewer said, "What you really need to do is take Tucker for an MRI. Immediately."

Now I was really scared.

Dianne, the receptionist, handed me photocopied directions to Massachusetts Veterinary Referral Hospital in Woburn, Massachusetts.

One of the veterinary technicians put Tucker on the back seat of my car, and off we went.

I drove off in tears, aware that one option that might be presented today could be euthanization, if he had a tumor on his spine. Home was on the way to the hospital, but I didn't stop. I headed directly to Woburn, pushing through late morning traffic.

Even though I had gotten no sleep the night before, keeping awake was not a problem. All I could think was that this could be the end of the line for Tucker. It had been only three years since we lost Sheena, and that pain was still with me every day.

Selfishly, I thought, "How am I going to live without a dog? Is it too soon to adopt again, or should I foster?" If I had to put my dog to sleep... No, not today. He's too young to die.

Photo: Samuels Studio, Inc. (used with permission)
Sheena (who wouldn't miss this face?)

I spent the drive from Village Animal Hospital to Massachu-setts Veterinary Referral Hospital, some twenty-fve miles, reflecting on Tucker's life and our relationship.

I recalled the day we met Tucker at the foster home, where my first words upon seeing him were, "He's gorgeous!" I thought about all his issues, all the training, and all the trips to K-Mart to buy yet another baby gate.

I thought about how much he enjoyed agility, especially the fun of grabbing, running off with, and eating the plastic marga-rine lids used as targets.

10

Or the time we were at an outdoor agility class, and Tucker was enthusiastically going through the tunnel, over the jumps, and across the dogwalk when, midcourse, he zoomed across the lawn, under the fence, and into the swimming pool. It was as if he'd been plotting his "escape" to the pool for when we'd all least expect it.

I remembered the charity walk through downtown Concord, where we were walking four or five abreast on the sidewalk. I had paused to dodge a parking meter, and Tucker shot across the sidewalk, stuck his head into the back pocket of a stroller, and gulped down, in one swallow, a peanut butter sandwich, wrapped in wax paper, in a brown paper bag. (Yes, bag, wax paper, and sandwich were gone in about the time it takes to sneeze.)

I realized that, aside from an ear infection or two, Tucker had always been a healthy dog. I thought about what a great dog he had developed into. But his fun personality had not been on display the past eighteen hours.

For the duration of the ride, I couldn't stop thinking that my recollections might become his eulogy.

At last, I arrived at the hospital's address.

There was no sign in front of the building, but I pulled around back to the loading area.

I phoned the hospital to tell them we had arrived. The receptionist said they were on the way to help me get Tucker out of the car.

I waited. And waited. By now I was frantic. I rang the buzzer. I waited. I rang the buzzer again. And waited.

A woman wearing business attire came to the door. I told her, "I have Tucker in the car. I was told to bring him to the loading area."

The woman flashed a sympathetic smile, "You want the animal hospital. They're across the street."

I pulled out of the parking lot and saw a huge sign, "Massachusetts Veterinary Referral Hospital," across the street with a you-can't-possibly-miss-it modern building. Yet I missed it. That's what no sleep and teary vision will do, but such was my state of mind.

Photo: Judy Wolff

How did I miss this sign?

12

Photo: Judy Wolff
And how did I miss this building?

I drove up to the entrance. A blur of people in scrubs loaded Tucker onto a gurney and wheeled him inside. After parking the car, I was led to an examination room while Tucker had more tests. I waited to learn what was wrong with him, whether it was curable, and whether he'd ever be coming home.

The ER veterinarian, Dr. Sarah Allen, presented the results of the x-rays. She said that Dr. Gena Silver, the neurologist, also gave Tucker a neurological exam. Dr. Silver found weakness in both legs, worse on the left. He had limited motor ability (bad) but had sensation (good). There was a lesion in the T3-L3 region of the spinal column.

The possible causes:

- Intervertebral disc disease (damaged cartilage, herniated disc, traumatic disc)
- A tumor in or around the spinal cord (the worst case scenario)
- Fibrocartilaginous embolism (FCE) or a blood clot

With a herniated disc or tumor, the patient typically exhibits pain when examined, and the condition worsens with time.

13

With an FCE, there is pain just once and not again. Tucker's symptoms fit this profile. The "good" part of an FCE, compared to a tumor or herniated disc, is that once it happens, it doesn't get worse, and it gradually gets better. Of the three possible diagnoses, FCE presents the best chance for recovery. The treatment is non-surgical, requiring time and care, with the potential for the dog to regain 80-95% capability over a period of six to eight weeks.

I asked Dr. Allen if my waiting a day to bring Tucker in for examination could have made his condition worse. She said, "It depends. Is he worse now than he was yesterday?"

"No. He's the same."

"There's your answer."

Whew, with emotions of fear and anxiety overwhelming me, I didn't need to add guilt.

Dr. Allen then explained that they would like to give Tucker an MRI, under anesthesia, after a chest x-ray and some bloodwork.

At some point, someone told me to go home, that Tucker was sedated and it would be some time until the neurologist saw him and reviewed the results of the x-rays and MRI. He would be staying overnight at the hospital, so I didn't need to wait.

I fidgeted at home. I emailed some friends about what was going on, but asked them not to call so I could leave the phone line open for the hospital to call me. I had totally forgotten about call waiting, and about the fact that the hospital had my cell phone number as well.

I needed to do something.

I drove to our veterinarian's office, because in the rush to get Tucker to the hospital, and with their consent, I hadn't yet paid for that morning's visit.

On the ride over, my cell phone rang. Dr. Silver was calling with results. The good news: they ruled out a tumor. I pulled over to the side of the road, scribbling notes, trying to think of what to ask.

Dr. Silver explained that Tucker had suffered a disc injury at L2-L3, consistent with FCE/traumatic disc. There was some compression on his left side, probably a tiny bit of hemorrhage (blood clot) pushing on the spinal cord. The compression was mild.

Then Dr. Silver said that the compression could be relieved with surgery. The procedure would be to drill a window in Tucker's spinal column to see and remove the compressing material. The prognosis was good. She also said that he could improve without surgery as the compression was mild.

Without surgery, there was a chance of more bleeding and the compression could get worse.

She could do the surgery today, now, before Tucker woke up from the anesthesia they had administered for his MRI.

"How risky is the surgery?" I asked.

"It's bread-and-butter, routine. But all surgery has risks."

I asked her again to confirm what I thought I had heard: he could do fine without surgery, as the majority of the injury was due to bruising, but may recover faster and more completely with surgery to remove the compressive material.

I had to decide within a few minutes, as Tucker was under anesthesia waiting on my decision.

I had been up with Tucker all night and was in no condition to authorize surgery that (1) might not be needed and (2) carried the risks inherent in any surgery.

Rehabilitation would be the same with or without surgery. He would stay in the hospital at least until the following night.

When he came home, I would need to confine him in a small area unless I could be there to support him. He would need support (with a sling) to walk. He would need physical therapy. He would have to rest for two weeks, just taking it easy. He could not be put into a crate because he shouldn't "horseshoe" (to turn around). No stairs for a while.

I told Dr. Silver that I would call her back in five minutes.

It took me a few minutes to continue my drive to Village Animal Hospital, where I spoke with Dr. Sophie Rush [*name changed on request*]. She was new to the practice and this was the first time I had met her. I told her my dog had suffered an FCE with some mild compression and that I needed to decide whether to operate.

What did she advise? I'm sure she loved being put in that position! She said if it were her dog, she'd go for the surgery. She added that the hospital Tucker was in was excellent.

Veterinarians advised, yes, operate. Yet my gut said not to do it; Tucker is not a good patient and does not tolerate pain well. Only I know my dog, and I didn't think surgery was right for him. It helped knowing that I could change my mind over the next two weeks.

I decided to postpone surgery for a couple of days to see how Tucker would do, since he had already made a little progress in the last 24 hours. (In fact, it was 3:00 P.M., exactly 24 hours since Tucker's injury.)

Dr. Silver said there was no urgent need to perform the surgery right away, and there was no harm in waiting (except for the increased cost of extra days in the hospital).

The deciding factor for me was that there was little risk of the compression getting worse, even if we waited up to two weeks.

I called Dr. Silver and told her that I wanted to wait on the surgery.

I also asked about chiropractic treatment and acupuncture. She said definitely no to chiropractic care. Acupuncture was something we could try later if I wanted, but in her opinion it was more helpful in treating *painful* spinal cord problems than with paralysis.

Paralysis. When Dr. Brewer had said the word earlier, it was just a word. Now that tests confirmed Tucker's condition, hearing the word was overwhelming.

I emailed an update to friends:

"Tucker has weakness in both hind legs.

He can bear weight on the right leg, enough to stand if supported with a sling, but his left leg is completely paralyzed, from the spine to the toes, with the foot knuckled under.

He has a little sensation in the left leg, so that is promising. He can move his tail a little but he cannot wag it.

No idea how much function he will regain, will have a better idea in two weeks.

No idea yet when Tucker will be home.

There will be a lot of supportive care over the next several weeks, the full extent of which hasn't hit home yet.

Meanwhile, it is so quiet here at home I don't know what to do with myself, am puttering aimlessly, can't concentrate on anything."

Home without a dog felt unnatural. I wondered how Tucker was doing, away from home, in a foreign place, surrounded by strangers, most of whom probably carried cat scent.

I called the hospital at 7:50 P.M. Amy, the nurse who would be taking care of him through the night, said he was doing fine, showing response. He was walking well with a sling, using his right leg but not his left. They'd be giving him a little food soon. He was alert, in no pain, and was happy to go on a walk and be out of his cage.

I went to bed, apprehensive of what life with a partially paralyzed dog would be like, but incredibly relieved that Tucker's condition was not life-threatening. My dog would live. The quality of his life was something we'd be able to gauge in a few weeks. But for today, it was enough to know that whatever felled him would not kill him.

3

WHAT IS AN FCE?

What is a fibrocartilaginous embolism?

The spinal column, in dogs as well as other animals (including humans) is made up of small bones, called vertebrae. Between each of these bones is a gel-filled capsule, called a disc, which cushions the vertebrae as the spine bends with movement.

The spinal column protects the spinal cord, which, along with the brain, forms the core of the nervous system. Nerves radiate from the spinal cord throughout the body; electrical impulses from the brain travel down the spinal cord and along the various pathways of nerve bundles. Signals from the brain travel through the nerves, enabling various functions. Among these functions are pain sensation and the recruitment of muscles for movement.

When a fibrocartilaginous embolism occurs, somehow a bit of the gelatinous material inside one of the vertebral discs leaks out and enters the circulatory system (bloodstream), causing an embolism (the technical term for a blood clot), which blocks the blood flow to the spinal cord. How and why this happens is unknown. But the damage that results is known: the spinal cord is injured, sometimes permanently.

There is currently no way to predict which dogs might be affected by a fibrocartilaginous embolism, and there is no way to prevent one.

The condition does not appear to be genetic, though some breeds (especially large and giant breeds) are afflicted more often than others. Young and middle-aged (three to six years), active dogs are more likely to be stricken.

At the time of an FCE, the dog is often participating in normal activity such as playing, running, or jumping and suddenly goes down, often with a yelp. Afterwards, the dog is unable to move one or more limbs, but does not exhibit pain.

Severity ranges from weakness to complete paralysis, and possibly incontinence. Weakness or paralysis can affect just one side of the body. The effect on an individual dog depends on precisely where along the spinal cord the embolism struck.

Typically, the condition stabilizes or improves over time; it does not worsen after the first 24 hours.

The degree of improvement over the first two weeks is often used to gauge how much mobility will be regained, but this timing is not absolute.

Signs consistent with an FCE would be acute paralysis, non-progressive (does not get worse after 12-24 hours), and non-painful.

Aside from autopsy, the only way to confirm FCE from disc herniation (which *can* present the same way) is by magnetic resonance imaging (MRI).

Treatment for a fibrocartilaginous embolism consists of physical therapy and time.

Can a human have an FCE? Apparently so, a quick Internet search shows, but it is exceedingly rare in people.

Soon after Tucker's FCE, I spoke with a breeder who told me that until fifteen or twenty years ago, all dogs with this condition were euthanized because it wasn't known that they could recover. But a few owners said they didn't care if their dogs were paralyzed and incontinent, they would wait and see. Those owners were really dedicated and courageous, because they had no reason to expect their dogs to improve. But some of their dogs did eventually get better, giving hope to people like myself.

In Tucker's case, he might have twisted his back suddenly while chasing the cat next door, though we can never know for sure.

What I have learned is that most people have never heard of a fibrocartilaginous embolism. For simplicity, I tell people an FCE is a stroke that affects the spinal column instead of the brain, and I use the colloquial "blood clot" instead of "embolism." "Spinal stroke" or just "stroke" is something people can understand better than fibrocartilaginous embolism. Not to mention, it's easier to pronounce. And spell.

21

Photo: Mary Hogan
The author with Sheena (left) and Tucker (right) in 2004

4

PREPARING THE HOUSE (TUESDAY) AND HOSPITAL DISCHARGE (WEDNESDAY)

Tucker's FCE happened on Sunday. Monday he was tested and admitted to the hospital, where he stayed overnight.

Tuesday morning, Tracy, one of the nurses, called with an update, "Tucker is doing OK, is ambulatory with a sling, dragging his left leg. He's eating and drinking, is bright and alert, and is happy to sniff around outside."

That afternoon, I visited Tucker at the hospital during his physical therapy evaluation. Tucker was showing some improvement since the day before. (Hooray!)

His right hind leg was strong enough to bear weight, so he was able to walk on three legs, assisted with a sling. His paralyzed left hind leg still had no motor ability. He walked on the top of the knuckled foot because he had no sense of where his foot was in space (no proprioception). Sadly, he couldn't wag his tail, because those nerves were affected, too. He didn't appear to be incontinent, a common concern with a spinal injury. He seemed to be in good spirits and appeared to have been treated well.

The physical therapy plan for the next two weeks was designed to stimulate the nerves in Tucker's left hind leg so that he could regain function.

After meeting with his physical therapist, I met with his neurologist, Dr. Gena Silver, for a prognosis. With aggressive physical therapy (at the hospital as an outpatient) and home care, Tucker had a good chance of "being functional on four legs" but she wouldn't and couldn't say what percent of function we might expect him to regain. A good sign was that he could feel deep pain in his left leg.

She said we should see progress in two weeks. If we didn't see progress in a month, it would be, Dr. Silver said, "depressing."

The only treatment for an FCE is physical therapy, rest, and time. Rehab could take six months, but first we needed to get through the next two weeks, at which time Dr. Silver would re-examine Tucker. At that time, we would know if he was progressing quickly enough through physical therapy, or if he would need the surgery for his disc compression to facilitate healing.

I told Dr. Silver that our next-door neighbors had seen Tucker turning and lunging after a cat that had wandered into their yard. That was moments before he cried out and went down. Dr. Silver said it was possible that the sudden twisting caused the spinal injury, but it was impossible to say with certainty how it happened. Given Tucker's animosity towards cats, my guess is that this cat wanted to even the score.

After the physical therapy evaluation and the briefing by the neurologist, I was ready to go home, alone. But surprise! The hospital was ready to discharge Tucker. While that would have been great news under most circumstances, I wasn't prepared.

Since I'd expected him to stay another night, I hadn't prepared the house for a disabled dog, nor had I cancelled my Tuesday evening strength training class.

Leaving Tucker to spend another night with his new best friends at the hospital, I drove home, taught my class, and spent three hours rearranging the house.

The areas of concern were confinement, access to the outside without using stairs, and traction on the floors. Here's how we dealt with each.

For confinement, the situation was that we had a dog with some restrictions and limited mobility, but enough mobility to get into trouble. Dr. Silver did not want Tucker to be crated, as he would have to horseshoe to turn around. I would supervise him as usual when I was home, but if I needed to leave the house, I would have to confine him, and in such a way that he couldn't reach anything edible. Edible, by Tucker's definition, is whatever fits in his mouth.

Photo: Judy Wolff

The set-up in the breezeway

We cleared everything off the breezeway that he could eat or trip over, set up his dog bed and a few safe toys, and set up an x-pen (a wire "playpen" but without a floor) positioned to block the loveseat so he wouldn't be tempted to climb up on it and risk falling or hyperextending his injured spine.

We placed the x-pen far enough away from the back door and window that he could see anyone looking through the glass without having to stand.

Then we braced the x-pen from tipping over if nudged. If a 75-lb dog was determined to knock the x-pen over, my money would be on the dog. The breezeway was sufficiently puppy-proof from objects small enough to swallow, but tripping over a fallen x-pen probably wasn't a designated physical therapy exercise.

An outdoor baby gate across the back stairs would discourage visitors and delivery people from approaching from the driveway. (Visitors would likely agitate or excite Tucker, and he needed rest.)

The ramp at the back door would be the easiest way for Tucker to get into and out of the house. When we needed the car, I could park next to the bottom of the ramp and assist Tucker into and out of the car to avoid using stairs.

Photo: Judy Wolff

The ramp

Tucker would need extra traction, so up from the basement came the rubber-backed mats that lined the hardwood and tile floors during Sheena's geriatric, arthritic, and incontinent days. Ugly? Yes. More importantly: they're inexpensive, effective, and machine-washable.

Photo: Judy Wolff
The nonskid mats covering the tiled floor

Photo: Judy Wolff
More nonskid mats to provide traction

After much trial and error, and after jockeying to find space in our small house for objects needing to be relocated, the house was ready for Tucker.

Tuesday night, I slept upstairs in my own bed, for what would be the last time in three months.

Wednesday, I arrived at the hospital in time for Tucker's first physical therapy treatment. (Yesterday's physical therapy session was just an evaluation.)

Charlie Evans, the physical therapist and certified canine rehabilitation therapist who would coordinate Tucker's rehabilitation, explained that function is lost in this order: proprioception (awareness of one's body in space), motor ability, superficial pain, and deep pain. Function is regained in the opposite order. Tucker still felt deep pain, but we had a lot of work ahead.

Charlie took Tucker through a series of passive range-of-motion exercises and stretches, explaining each one to me so that I could do them at home.

I would be doing range-of-motion exercises for his knee (stifle), ankle (tarsus), shoulder, and elbow. I would also be stretching his hip flexors, hamstrings, quadriceps, biceps, triceps, and shoulder.

Most importantly, I would be stretching his toe flexors six times a day, three sets of one-minute stretches per session. The toe flexors were the muscles that were curled under, in that knuckled position.

Charlie pointed out that I might have difficulty getting Tucker to flip over to stretch his other side, since Tucker resisted lying on his left side because he knew he couldn't get up by himself using that leg.

Then Charlie took Tucker into a tank that filled with water—an underwater treadmill. The underwater treadmill would help build strength and improve proprioception.

29

Charlie showed me other equipment that they would be using: e-stim (electrical stimulation), laser therapy, Cavaletti rails, and balance boards. Very cool stuff.

The home instructions from physical therapy were detailed and ran for several pages:

- Massage Tucker twice a day, following detailed instructions on various massage strokes, with emphasis on the paralyzed leg, from hip to toes.

- Take him for walks of five to ten minutes on various surfaces, four or five times a day for bathroom breaks. Walking on different terrain would help stimulate his nerves. When possible, walk him on grass or gravel (rather than asphalt) to prevent abrasions on the knuckled foot. If he had to walk on asphalt, protect his foot with a boot.

- When trimming his nails, keep the ones on his knuckled foot longer so they will not wear down to the quick.

- Keep him quiet and confined when not doing his therapy exercises.

- Practice having him stand for thirty seconds a few times a day.

- Do passive range-of-motion exercises twice a day.

- Stretch all four legs twice a day. Stretch the foot that knuckles six times a day, for three sets of a minute each.

- While Tucker is standing to eat, challenge his balance by making him sway and rock, but don't let him reposition his feet.

- Elevate his food and water dishes about a foot off the floor to force him to shift his weight to his hind legs.

- Anytime his foot knuckles, flex it to the correct position. (It would be a steady job keeping that foot positioned.)

- Stimulate the nerves in his leg as much as possible: play "footsie," tickle his toes, spread his toes, and tap a finger up and down his leg.

Swimming? Not yet. For now, walking would be better because it is a weight-bearing exercise. Besides, dogs use their front legs more when swimming; Tucker needed to work his hind legs.

Charlie showed me how to support Tucker's back end with a sling, get Tucker up and down stairs, and into and out of the car. For now, so that he wouldn't extend his back too much, we were not to allow Tucker to climb up flights of stairs, just the few steps he needed to ascend to get into the hospital would be enough.

Before leaving the hospital, I met briefly with Dr. Silver for Tucker's discharge orders. Dr. Silver reiterated some of the instructions I had just heard in physical therapy: all activity should be controlled, no running (as if!), and Tucker should have both his front and back supported when standing. Tucker and I were to see Dr. Silver again in two weeks, unless Tucker got worse.

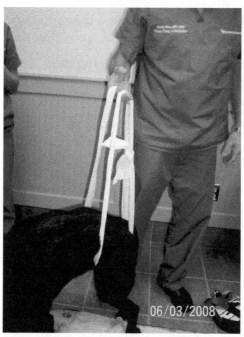

Photo: Judy Wolff

Supporting Tucker with a sling

I showed Dr. Silver and Charlie photographs of the setup at home: the ramp, rubber floor mats, and x-pen, and I got the green light to take Tucker home.

We got home Wednesday, around dinnertime, and I introduced Tucker to his new digs in the breezeway. He was just fine with the change and, as much as he seemed to enjoy his buddies at the hospital, was quite happy to be home; even happier to have dinner. ("Oh, boy, dog food again!")

I had expected to catch up on a lot of reading while sitting quietly with Tucker. Sure. I suspected the at-home care would take some time. It took some time, and then some. It's a good thing my schedule was flexible so that I could be home most of the day and follow through.

Wednesday night we started to get used to walking Tucker with the sling to help him around. Getting him outside to pee was an adventure, and then getting him to "go" when outside was even more of a challenge. I would need to learn how to take him out on my own.

Our instructions were that his walks should be controlled: leash in front and support in back. An octopus might have handled this task with aplomb. For these rookies with four hands between us, another pair of hands would have been useful to hold the leash, adjust the slipping booty, and position the ever-knuckling foot.

I slept downstairs with Tucker, on a twin-sized air mattress in the living room. So that Tucker couldn't get out during the night without awakening me, I wedged the mattress between the coffee table and loveseat, and put a baby gate at the foot of the bed. The only way Tucker could get out of bed would be to step on me. A 75-lb dog stepping on my head would certainly wake me.

It was a cozy arrangement.

Photo: David Wolff

Cozy sleeping arrangement:
Baby gate, sofa, and coffee table block Tucker in.
On the table is a camping light. A sling is on the floor.

5

THE TWO-WEEK VIGIL

We had made it through the initial shock, testing and diagnosis, and hospital discharge. Tucker was home. I was armed with a sheaf of written instructions, and I was overwhelmed by all the new additions to our daily routine. The two-week countdown had started.

During these two weeks, Tucker would return to the hospital for twice-a-week physical therapy sessions, in addition to his daily at-home therapy. After the initial two weeks, he would continue to have physical therapy once a week for several more months.

I cancelled all plans for the next two weeks, except for the Red Sox game that Saturday afternoon with Lois. It was to be the first game I had tickets for in many years. My husband would be home that day and, if necessary, the dog walker could stop by.

Our first day at home, getting used to a new routine, was tough, because of the various new challenges and logistical problems we needed to solve. Once we got the routine down, everything would be easier. I hoped.

I was fortunate to have a great support network.

The first week, I didn't leave the house, except to take Tucker to physical therapy. "We" (my sanity and I) are fortunate to have a mature, reliable, and responsible dog walker, Kathy Murphy. As a bonus, she has had experience caring for dogs with mobility issues, including another Lab, Sophie, paralyzed by an FCE. By the second week, Kathy visited with Tucker daily. Each day, before leaving the house, I would leave Kathy a detailed note about Tucker's activity and progress from the previous day. She, in turn, would write about what she did and how Tucker responded.

Kathy and I followed a military-precise schedule. Kathy would arrive at the house a half hour after my scheduled departure, and would spend a half hour with Tucker, taking him outside for a potty break, giving him a massage, and doing some of the stimulation exercises. She would also talk to him and give him lots of loving. Tucker adores her, even if she does call him a monkey. (She is also one of four people who call Tucker her boyfriend. Maybe I should rename him Tiger?)

I would return home no more than a half-hour after Kathy left. In this way, I would have an hour and a half for a speedy workout and a brief errand. No lingering at the gym to chat, no browsing in the store. If ever I was focused...

Kathy put me in touch with one of her clients, Cheryl, whose sweet yellow Lab, Sophie, had experienced a more severe FCE than Tucker, several years earlier.

Sophie's FCE affected her from the rib cage down. She had completely lost all function of both hind legs initially but was eventually able to resume walking and running, with a slightly odd gait. She never regained her ability to climb a full flight of stairs, but was able to do a few steps at a time to get on or off of their back deck. Overall, it was encouraging to hear how much progress they were able to make in a relatively short time.

Cheryl, a former occupational therapist, offered to show me some exercises that she did with Sophie to supplement those prescribed by Sophie's physical therapist. She said these were similar exercises to what she used to do with human stroke patients, adapted for canine anatomy and personality.

The support network kept ideas flowing.

Tucker's dog trainer, Kathy Fardy of Dog's Time, who had introduced me to clicker training soon after I adopted Tucker, suggested:

> "When my dogs had TPLO [*for torn ACL*] surgeries
> I did a lot of clicker lying-down games to keep their
> minds active and to help mentally tire them out.
> You are very good at that."

A few weeks later, when Tucker's dog walker went on vacation, his doggy daycare, Gemini Dogs, agreed to make special accommodations for him.

I emailed friends asking for advice and to borrow mobility gear. Someone on the freecycle.org list offered a Bottom's-Up Leash™, but she lived too far away. Someone else told me about websites for handicapped pets, and another recommended an aquatic therapy facility.

The Massachusetts Veterinary Referral Hospital professional and support staff were fabulous. They kept me and our veterinarian informed. They returned phone calls. They answered my many questions, and never made me feel stupid or that I was wasting their time.

Walking into the hospital, we always felt welcomed: the receptionist greeted us by name: "Tucker" and "Tucker's mom" (the only identity that mattered). At first, and for several visits until Tucker was able to walk the distance, I would need to drive up to the front door, walk Tucker to the reception desk, and ask the receptionist to watch him while I parked the car. Likewise, when we left the hospital, Tucker would stay with his friends in reception until I brought the car to the front door. Tucker loved the staff, even those who didn't give him cookies. (But especially the people who did.)

The only part of the hospital experience I can't say that I enjoyed was the cost, though throughout the experience, my only thought was that it would be worth it if Tucker could walk again.

I don't know how I would have managed without everyone's help and emotional support. These days were physically and mentally exhausting. I was worried, fatigued, and anxious. Tucker was mellow, cooperative, and hungry.

On Thursday, the day after Tucker's discharge from the hospital, after just one day of home care, I wrote in an email to a friend:

> "I am already in need of respite care. At least I know that this is a condition that can improve and he has a chance of walking again. I don't know how people manage who are caring for people with no hope of recovery or whose conditions are expected to worsen over time. At least I can expect better times ahead."

For this two-week period, we settled into a routine. We did the first set of exercises during Tucker's breakfast, the ones where I rocked him gently from side-to-side and front-to-back. Then we went outside for a brief walk. When we returned, with muscles warmed up from the brief exercise, I would give Tucker a massage and do his range-of-motion and stretching exercises.

Day-to-day logistics worked out about as planned.

The wooden ramp in the front worked well enough to get Tucker to the street and driveway. I would have loved another ramp from the deck to the backyard for more convenient and private potty breaks. I inquired about using a portable plastic ramp for access to the backyard, or to help Tucker get in and out of the car, but the physical therapist said it was too narrow.

So we used the wooden ramp in the front to go outside, and we walked around the house and through the gate to the back-yard. Or we went through the garage to the yard, to avoid stairs. (We were eventually able to use the plastic ramp in the back, but only for a few months. Before the first snowstorm, we garaged the plastic ramp and moved the wooden ramp from the front to the back, where it has stayed for more than a year.)

Photo: Judy Wolff
The portable plastic ramp. It would be several weeks before Tucker was able to use it.

Getting Tucker into the car was easier than getting him out. I would give him a boost onto the floor and from there, would assist him onto the seat. The first time, Tucker looked up, wondering how he would perform his customary leap onto the back seat. I told him, "Do it like Sheena," and, smart boy, he put his front paws on the floor and waited for me to help him up. Tasks like this are so much easier when the dog cooperates!

I didn't expect getting Tucker out of the car to be a problem. Since the only places he would be going these days was to the veterinarian's office or physical therapy, there would be someone at the other end to help. As it turned out, I got the hang of helping him out of the car in a day.

I had bought a Bottom's-Up Leash™ because I thought its padding might be more comfortable for Tucker. It tended to slip down his legs; the physical therapist confirmed that it was adjusted properly. But I quickly lost patience with constantly repositioning it—a shame because its red and black coloring coordinated so nicely with his collar and harness. The homemade sling was much easier to use and faster to put on. In fairness to the Bottom's-Up Leash™, it's a great-looking product, but probably better suited for short intervals of use, such as going up a flight of stairs.

It was recommended that I get a product called Show Foot™ to spray on the bottom of Tucker's feet a few times a week to add traction. I actually already had two cans, left over from when Sheena had difficulty with traction on the kitchen floor. It didn't help her traction, but it made it easier for her to leave sticky, dirty footprints everywhere. (Now I know the secret: spray it on when the dog is tired and lying down, and let it dry for several minutes before letting the dog stand.) Tucker didn't like the sensation of having his feet sprayed. He resisted the spray on three feet; he couldn't feel it on the paralyzed leg.

We also had the Battle of the Boots. The boots fell off. The boots wore off. The boots got stinky from being dragged through puddles of dog urine. But the boots were essential. The boot protected the dragging foot from abrasions and excessive wear of the nails. Naturally, the boot would slip off every few steps. The challenge was to put the boot back on while holding the sling under his hips so he wouldn't fall. All while holding a leash in front.

Over the next few weeks, Tucker wore out eight boots. The first four were doggy snow boots that I had once bought to protect Tucker's paws from road salt and ice balls. We used them just one time in the snow, because they fell off every few steps. We used them now only because we had them already and needed something to protect Tucker's foot. A few days of scuffing wore a hole large enough to render each of them useless.

One day, while we were walking across the driveway, Tucker's boot fell off and was lying behind him, out of my reach. Should I set him down on the hot asphalt? Would this very bored dog decide to take himself for a walk, um, hop? How could I reach the boot and put it on him? Neighbors drove past. I wondered what they were thinking. This must have looked quite odd. Somebody finally stopped and retrieved the boot for me.

The next set of four boots I found as markdowns in the bargain room at a pet supply warehouse, where Tucker was welcome to come in and try them on for size. They were adorable: a shimmery silver with a center zipper. Very sharp looking—if you like the disco look—and they fit quite well. Alas, these too wore out in a few days.

Photo: Judy Wolff

Tucker's disco boot

On the recommendation of the physical therapist, I ordered custom boots from Tammy and Teddy's, a business that specializes in boots for dogs with spinal injuries. Because they were made to fit Tucker's foot and ankle exactly, using measurements of paw circumference, length, height, and width, these boots fit snugly and securely. Tucker's boots are red with black trim, to match his other accessories (collar, leash, harness). We call these his "boo-tays" (emphasis on the second syllable) because they are elegant.

One of the day-to-day challenges that proved more annoying than expected was getting Tucker to pee. At his hospital discharge, I was told that Tucker's metabolism had slowed down from inactivity, so I shouldn't expect him to urinate as much as usual. He was hardly going at all; at one point it was nineteen hours between voiding.

I still gave him plenty of opportunities, because he was not communicating a need to go out, and he was having accidents in the house.

The first few days I was home alone with Tucker, each bathroom trip was an adventure. We didn't have the rhythm/coordination of walking more than a step or two at a time with all the gear (sling, boot, leash). One day in particular I was having more difficulty than usual, having been outside for a while with no potty results. The only neighbor I found at home was an athletic twenty-year-old, used to handling horses, and even she gave up, exhausted, after a few minutes.

Each of these challenges—ramps, car, sling, boots, and bathroom—were problems only until I found a solution. Once the puzzle was solved, no big deal.

The next challenge was remembering to do all the exercises. When one day blurs into the next, it's hard to keep track.

I thought keeping track of the home exercises we had done each day would be easier with a checklist of some kind.

Tucker's Therapy

What to Do	Frequency	Reps/Duration	When to Do	Comment	Last Done
Massage	2x per day		After outside walk	Hydrate before and after	
PROM	2x per day	10-15 reps	After massage or walk or heat pack		
Stretch	2x per day	15-30 seconds	After walk or heat pack		
Stretch toe flexors	6x per day	3 reps, at least 1 minute each	After walk		
Walk	5x per day	5-10-15 min.		Use sling or Bottoms-Up, with leash in front. Boot on Left rear foot. Vary surfaces.	
Weight shifting	2-3x per day	5-10 reps	Mealtime	Elevate food & water	
Stand	3-4x per day	30-60 seconds	Mealtime		
Downward compression	2-3x per day	5-10 reps	Mealtime		
Check foot	Regularly			Abrasions, wearing of nail	Sat. p.m
Apply Show Foot	2x week				

Other things to do throughout the day:
- Massage or rub his leg, toes to hip
- Tickle and spread his toes
- Tap up and down his leg
- Play footsie

The daily log for recording Tucker's exercises

I created a table that listed the exercises and frequency, and provided boxes to check off as we did each one. (I revised this table several times as Tucker's home program was modified to keep pace with his progress.)

I continued to take notes obsessively. How obsessively? Every time he went to the bathroom, either in my presence or for the dog walker, we recorded what he did and the time of day, for an entire month.

Note-taking provided an outlet for my anxiety and provided a distraction from the ever-pressing questions: Would Tucker ever walk again? If he didn't, would his quality of life be diminished so much that I would consider letting him go? Time would answer those questions. (Yes, and no.)

Before the first week was up, Tucker started licking his paw, a good sign that he was feeling nerve pain or tingling in that leg.

During that week, Tucker had several visitors to cheer him.

Photo: Judy Wolff
Tucker playing piano for Will, then eleven months, and his mom, Beth, exactly one week after his FCE.

How did the physical therapy go during those two weeks?

On June 7, six days after the FCE, Tucker showed promising signs in physical therapy. Charlie was walking him on the underwater treadmill. The way this worked is that Charlie and Tucker would enter the tank, and an assistant would press the button to fill the tank with water. When the water reached the right level, Charlie would activate the treadmill's belt. He would grasp Tucker's hind legs and move them in the pattern of a walk.

On this day, Charlie could feel muscle tone—a little mobility and some muscular contraction—in the upper thigh. Tucker was also knuckling less on his foot. Then, after his morning massage, Tucker gave a full tail wag! We could see his quadriceps muscle twitching. Also, in the previous 24 hours, Tucker had started nibbling and licking his paralyzed leg, which could mean he felt a sort of pins-and-needles sensation. Charlie said his progress was good.

07/19/2008

Photo: Judy Wolff

Tucker on the underwater treadmill

Photo: *Judy Wolff*
Tucker enjoying walking on the underwater treadmill

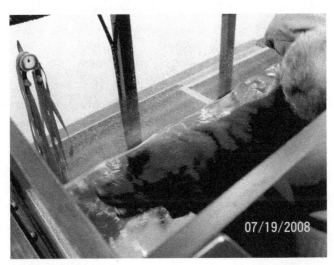

Photo: *Judy Wolff*
Tucker on the underwater treadmill, from above

His next physical therapy session was scheduled for Tuesday, to be followed by his first acupuncture treatment. Charlie thought Tucker would benefit greatly from acupuncture, and I agreed enthusiastically, as acupuncture had brought enormous relief for Sheena's arthritis.

Acupuncture on dogs (and other animals) is similar to acupuncture on people: a trained, licensed practitioner inserts hair-thin, sterile needles in precise locations on the body to facilitate the flow of Qi (or Chi), the life energy. The client rests with the needles in place for about twenty minutes, and the needles are removed.

Dr. Beth Innis, who treated Tucker with acupuncture, is a licensed veterinarian with additional training in acupuncture. She would start each session by giving Tucker a brief exam, and by interviewing me about his mood, behavior, and physical state since our last visit. Tucker would lay on a blanket on the floor. Then she would insert the needles, making sure the wrappers were out of the reach of Mr. Dietary Indiscretion. When the needles were in place, she would leave Tucker to rest, under my supervision. He usually stayed on the blanket, though at least once per session he would get up to show me where on the counter the cookie jar could be found.

Tucker loved his acupuncture treatments almost as much as he loved seeing Dr. Beth. He loved her even when cookies weren't involved.

Photo: Judy Wolff

Tucker with Dr. Beth

We decided to discharge him from acupuncture at the point (pun intended) that he started to remove the needles himself as soon as Dr. Beth left the examination room. By then, four months after his FCE, Tucker had made significant progress healing and just needed to build strength.

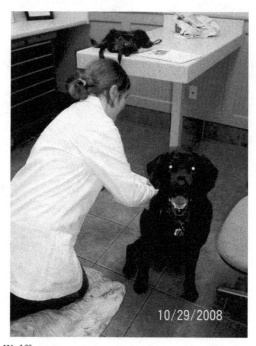

Photo: Judy Wolff
Tucker getting acupuncture needles inserted

Photo: Judy Wolff
Tucker tasting acupuncture needles

While it was encouraging seeing progress, it was also exhausting.

The next day, Sunday, a week after the FCE, I emailed a friend:

> "I'm pretty tired. The only time I've been out of the house since Wednesday has been to take Tucker to PT yesterday. I've been out of bed since 5:45 A.M. (I'll spare you details, but it involves Tucker and the need to launder the sheets of the air mattress we were sharing.)"

One night during the second week, Tucker licked his paw so aggressively while I slept that he developed a hot spot. The twin-sized air mattress Tucker and I shared was cozy; add an Elizabethan collar and the sleeping arrangement became snug.

Photo: David Wolff
Tucker with his Elizabethan collar

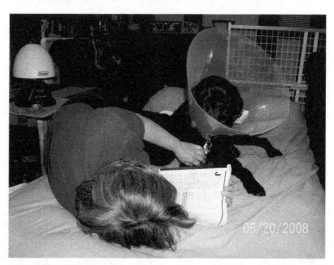

Photo: David Wolff
Sleeping with the Conehead

An exciting milestone occurred on day 12 after the FCE: the Show Foot™ spraying elicited a movement. Tucker jerked his leg back from the hip when spritzed. Yeah, it was a reflex, but *any* sign of life in that limb was exciting.

Tucker made some progress the first few days of physical therapy, but then hit a wall. The physical therapist described his progress after one session as "fast," but a few days later, when no further progress materialized, as "slow." He wouldn't be more specific as to what to expect in terms of recovery because "every case is different."

Nearing the end of the two weeks, Tucker could put some weight on that leg but could not move it voluntarily. The most promising signs were some muscle tone in his thigh, and occasional leg twitches when he slept. At this point, I was happy to see any movement, and I was desperate to see some advancement.

On June 15, two weeks after the FCE, I decided to capitalize on those involuntary twitches. One afternoon, during our stretches, Tucker's leg twitched and he "pulled" the leg back as I held onto his foot. He wasn't really pulling; it was a reflex, but I figured I had nothing to lose, and "clicked" the motion.

Let me explain: Tucker and I have done some clicker training, which is a teaching method that uses a marker to tell the learner (in this case, the dog) that whatever he just did is "right" and that he would get rewarded for that behavior (with a treat, playtime, or whatever the learner finds rewarding). The marker precisely captures the moment when the learner performs a desired act. The marker I use is a plastic device that makes a "clicking" sound when I press its button.

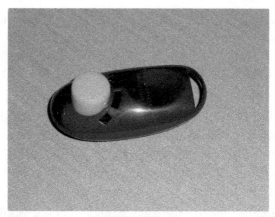

Photo: Judy Wolff

The clicker

Clicker training is based on the scientific principles of oper-ant conditioning (as in B.F. Skinner's research). Karen Pryor, a behavioral biologist, pioneered the use of operant conditioning, in the form of clicker training, in animals of all species—marine mammals, rhinoceroses, birds, cats, fish, horses, rabbits, chick-ens—you name it.

I remember once reading an article Karen Pryor had written proposing a theory that clicker training was so effective because the click was processed immediately by the amygdala, the primi-tive ("reacting") part of the brain, instead of going through the cortex for processing ("thinking").

(A year after Tucker's spinal injury, Karen Pryor's *Reaching the Animal Mind* was published. A fascinating read, the book has an interesting chapter on the clicker and neuroscience, in which she elaborates on learning, the physiology of the brain, and clicker training.)

So, I wondered, could I "connect" directly to Tucker's brain with the clicker, to stimulate his brain to send the signal down his spinal column to the bundle of nerves that activated the mus-cles in his leg? Maybe it would help. If not, it wouldn't hurt.

Would using the clicker to mark any movement of the leg let Tucker "learn" that movement, for which I would reward him with a treat? His "learning" would not be a conscious activity. I'm sure if he could have moved that leg voluntarily, he would have, because, well, it would have been easier for him. But if somehow a click would juice his brain to say, "Hey buddy, move the leg," we'd have a leg up on the rehab. (Sorry, stupid pun.)

What did I have to lose? At worst, I might create some confusion about the clicker and potentially slow down our previous training. I wasn't worried; clicker training is so forgiving that we'd recover from a minor setback. It was more important for Tucker to walk.

So on June 15, Tucker twitched. I clicked and gave him a treat. Twitch, click, treat. Twitch, click, treat. The twitching seemed to get progressively stronger; each time Tucker retracted his leg, I'd hold it harder. We played tug of war with the leg.

Did the clicker help? Since this was by no means a valid scientific experiment with acceptable methodology or even as much as a control group, I can't say. What I observed is that Tucker started to show results around the time I reinforced his movements with the clicker.

But we were using lots of different methods that week. I wasn't trying to prove anything; I was just desperate to get my dog walking again. The use of the clicker in this way did nothing to diminish our later training and our relationship. So maybe it helped, maybe it didn't, but it did no harm.

Closing in on the end of the two-week period of "conservative management" (no surgery), Tucker continued with physical therapy and acupuncture. I still continued to click and treat any leg movement. Even though it appeared as if he had plateaued, I was hoping for a breakthrough.

We got that breakthrough (*drumroll, please*) the morning of Tucker's follow-up appointment with the neurologist. Dr. Silver was very pleased with, and pleasantly surprised by, Tucker's progress in the two weeks since she had last seen him.

Before stepping into the examination room, she had read the physical therapy report, written 24 hours earlier and already outdated. Tucker's mobility showed enough improvement that Dr. Silver didn't mention surgery, except once, to say that she thought he'd heal faster with it, but could possibly do just as well without.

Dr. Silver set realistic long-term expectations: Tucker probably wouldn't regain 100% of his pre-FCE abilities, but 90-95% was possible; time would tell.

She said his incontinence could be from the spinal injury. Whether it would resolve itself was something we'd just need to wait and see. (Several weeks later I had Tucker tested for a urinary tract infection, which turned out to be the culprit. Antibiotics cured the infection, and the accidents stopped. Funny thing is, under normal circumstances, I would have had him tested for a urinary tract infection as a first step, but under the circumstances, I attributed the incontinence to the spinal injury.)

Wait and see: the theme for the next six months.

6

REHAB (THE FIRST SIX MONTHS)

With the most critical period having passed, we needed to continue to build Tucker's strength. The long-term goal was to get Tucker to where he could walk thirty minutes at a stretch.

But at this point, Tucker still wasn't walking at all.

We continued physical therapy, as an outpatient and at home.

At physical therapy, Tucker would be led onto a wobble board, and Charlie, his physical therapist, would rock the board in several directions while Tucker would need to balance to keep from falling off.

Walking on the underwater treadmill continued. Tucker thoroughly enjoyed being in the water (though he'd rather swim in it) and, being a Labrador Retriever goofball, had enormous fun splashing Charlie from head-to-toe. He especially enjoyed the part where he would come out of the tank and shake himself off on everyone.

Another exercise at physical therapy used Cavaletti rails. These are a set of PVC rods horizontally spaced at fixed intervals. The objective was for Tucker to walk from one end to the other, while picking up his hind legs.

Tucker was familiar with the exercise from his agility classes: because dogs don't pay attention to their hind legs, a similar drill called the "ladder" is one of the first exercises dogs learn in agility training.

With agility, as with physical therapy, the goal is proprioception, or body awareness.

In these early weeks, Tucker's walk through the Cavaletti rails went something like this: step forward lifting front left leg and then right hind leg, then right front leg, and thunk. The "thunk" was the left hind leg dragging behind, whacking the rail. *Step, step, step, thunk. Step, step, step, thunk.*

Photo: Judy Wolff
Tucker walking through the Cavaletti rails

Photo: Judy Wolff
Tucker walking through the Cavaletti rails

After his workout, Tucker would be stretched and massaged.

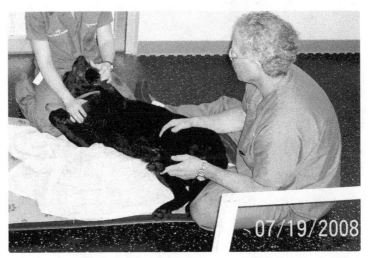

Photo: Judy Wolff
Massage at physical therapy

As you can see, he enjoyed the sensation and attention.

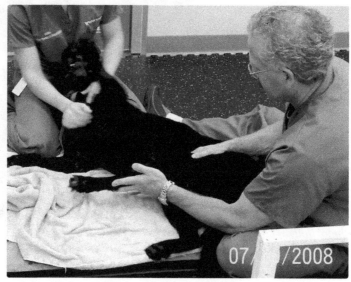

Photo: Judy Wolff
More massage at physical therapy

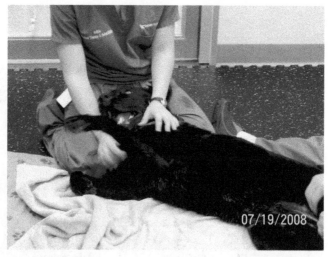

Photo: Judy Wolff
Stretching at physical therapy

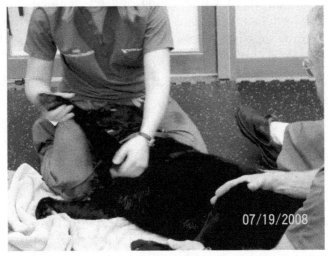

Photo: Judy Wolff
More stretching at physical therapy

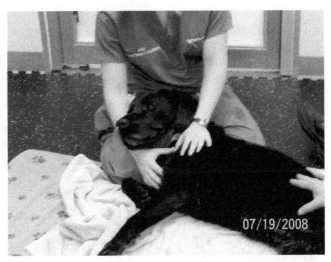

Photo: Judy Wolff
Relaxed from massage & stretching at physical therapy

At home, we continued the massage and stretches, with special emphasis on toe flexors. We continued playing footsie, having Tucker stand while eating and challenging his balance with forward/backward and side-to-side swaying, downward compression, passive range of motion exercises, foot/leg tapping, and short walks (assisted by the sling).

Movement of any kind, even involuntary twitching, was still cause for celebration.

Three weeks after the FCE, Tucker had gradually regained some muscle tone and nerve signal to the leg, at least as far as the thigh. He was able to bear weight on the left hind leg and walk very short distances without support from a sling. His foot still knuckled under.

His gait was all from the hip; he dragged the lower part of his leg. Think of Chester, from the TV western *Gunsmoke*. (If you're too young to remember this show, watch the videos on the Internet.)

From time to time, I would observe a slight movement at the knee.

When Tucker moved, he was *fast*. Three weeks after his FCE, Tucker took off while his dog walker was putting his boot back on. He was on a mission to visit the neighbor across the street who sometimes gives him cookies. Dogs are amazingly resilient about three-legged walking, especially when treats are involved.

Tucker's mood was good, and his normal personality finally returned. Tucker did not care about what he could *not* do; he did what he could and that was that.

For the first three weeks after the FCE, Tucker did not ask to go out even once for bathroom breaks, so I took him out every couple of hours and hoped to get lucky. Sometimes we were lucky, and sometimes we had a cleanup in aisle 3. He seemed aware that he was eliminating when he would start to "go" inside; his early-warning system apparently was on the fritz.

It was a month before he asked to go out. I was elated when he rang the bells by the back door. I quickly put on his booty and leash, and we went out. Tucker didn't need a potty break after all; he just wanted to visit the carpenters working next door. That summer, our neighbors on both sides were remodeling. Tucker took turns visiting each crew, where the guys would lavish him with belly rubs and comment on his daily progress.

Closing in on the one-month mark, the hot spot that developed from his chewing the foot was almost healed. The pins-and-needles sensation must have subsided.

Our routine was mildly disrupted when our dog walker went on vacation. Most days, I could arrange to be home nearly all day, but there are certain appointments one has to keep.

I didn't want to leave Tucker at home for several hours, so I discussed his situation with his daycare center, Gemini Dogs. (This daycare also had Sophie, the yellow Lab who had a severe FCE, as a client.) Gemini was willing to make accommodations for him, despite his restrictions and special needs: he would need assistance walking with the sling, he wasn't allowed to play with other dogs, he couldn't be crated, and he couldn't be left in their office, where there were papers and dog food. And possibly the distraction of the lovely Sophie. (Tucker likes blondes of any species, human, yellow Labs, and Golden Retrievers.)

Here's the response from Michelle Borelli, owner of Gemini Dogs, when I emailed the long list of special instructions for Tucker's stay:

> "I agree that an x-pen would be a better set-up for Tucker...we can place him in a pen in the office so that he doesn't have far to go to get outside, and like Sophie, if he does accidentally go inside, then it's nothing a little germicide won't fix!
>
> We can assign someone to massage his leg for him, although we shouldn't have to twist any arms for that job!

I will notify the staff about his condition and make sure that they know to set up a pen for him in the office...then you can let us know if there are any other special instructions other than what you mentioned here.

With Sophie, I think they give her the chance to go out every hour or so, in between each run of dogs. We could do the same with Tucker."

Tucker had some successful visits at daycare. But most days we both stayed home and worked on the rehab exercises.

For Tucker's rehabilitation, I was willing to try any method, as long as it bore no risk of causing further injury. I have no doubt that the conventional physical therapy was the key ingredient in Tucker's rehab, but other methods added the spices that flavored the dish.

Tucker's therapy included conventional physical therapy, acupuncture, the use of clicker training (described previously), and one more therapy: Reiki.

Reiki, pronounced *ray-kee,* means "universal life form energy." Originating in Japan, Reiki is a form of spiritual healing, a restorative and relaxing treatment practiced at holistic health centers and used in many hospitals for pre-operative and post-operative complementary care, as well as in hospice. While Reiki is spiritual, it has no belief system other than a general sense of harmony and peace from a mind-body connection.

What happens during a Reiki session? Not much, to the observer. With the client lying down, the Reiki practitioner lays hands at various places on the client's body (usually head, shoulder, stomach, and feet). A person receiving Reiki remains fully clothed. There is no massage or pressure involved, just light touch; sometimes the practitioner's hands hover above the client without touching. The hands are held in position for a period of time, ranging from three to ten minutes. The client might feel temperature changes, a radiant glow, tingling, a release of tension, and deep relaxation.

On June 20 and 21, Tucker had hands-on Reiki by two practitioners. Gale Lyman, a friend from the Lab Rescue Board, had an appointment in a neighboring town and offered to stop by and give Tucker a treatment. We had already scheduled a Reiki session with Aileen D'Angelo, referred by Sophie's mom, Cheryl, for the following day. Tucker loved both Gale and Aileen. He also loved the attention, the energy, and the gentle touch involved with Reiki.

Gale and our mutual friend, Deanna Smith, another Reiki master, both offered to give Tucker "distance Reiki." I can't explain it—and with energy healing you go with the flow and do not try to intellectualize the process. As I understand it, Reiki energy is not bound by space, so a Reiki master can channel the universal energy even at a distance. Do I believe it works? Why not? It couldn't do any harm, and my friends offered Tucker this service for free.

Coincidence or not, believe whatever you wish, but the sequence of events unfolded this way: Tucker's Reiki sessions were Friday and Saturday. After Saturday's Reiki session, while I was stretching his leg extensor muscles, Tucker uncurled his foot, a movement so rare at the time that I was jotting down all occurences. The following Tuesday, a little more than three weeks since the FCE, on June 24, Tucker had his weekly physical therapy session.

On that day, I emailed friends to play "Tucker *Jeopardy!*" with just this one "answer":

"Wow!"

The Question: What did the physical therapist say when he saw Tucker walk this afternoon?

He saw *significant* improvement since the previous week, said that Tucker was moving the entire leg voluntarily *and* had conscious proprioception of the left foot, for the first time since his FCE.

That Tucker was able to position his foot correctly—even after Charlie moved it—indicated that for the first time he has conscious proprioception. Proprioception is the last thing that comes back after a spinal injury, so this was excellent news.

I told Charlie that I thought the combination of physical therapy and acupuncture helped. I also mentioned how I used the clicker. We chatted a bit about holistic medicine and the reticence of veterinarians (and physicians) to use holistic methods. I confessed that Tucker had received two Reiki sessions the previous weekend, whereupon Charlie placed his hands on Tucker for more Reiki.

If I could have trained Tucker to help his therapy in any way, it would have been to teach him to reposition himself, without my having to move him into place. It was especially hard for me to move him without kneeling (bum knee); turning a 75-lb dog without his cooperation was difficult.

One night during this period, Tucker had one of those "only a Lab" moments that my friend Deanna has not stopped guffawing about with her Laughter Hall of Fame "Haw-haw-haw."

In the middle of the night, around 3:00 A.M., Tucker wriggled out of bed, crawling over me, with a sense of urgency.

In those days he was doing that "Chester" walk, dragging the left hind leg behind him. Under normal circumstances, you wouldn't call his movement "walking," but these were not normal circumstances. Tucker could get around, but it was a lot of work.

I hoisted myself up from the air mattress and followed him.

I assumed he had to use the restroom facilities, and, sure enough, he nosed the hanging bells, his signal to go out. I opened the door to the breezeway. Tucker made a beeline to…the dog food container. He sniffed it, turned around, and went back inside and to bed.

He must have had a nightmare that his food had gone away, and he needed to check on it. Reassured that his food was still there, he could sleep in peace.

And so the first month came and went.

As of July 1, the physical therapy goals were to build strength and endurance, improve function, and increase range-of-motion.

Tucker's new exercises included partial sit-stand exercises (like a half-squat), walking in circles, walking in figure-8 patterns, weaving, and stepping over Cavaletti rails.

I scrounged the basement and garage to improvise equipment. For Cavaletti rails, an old wooden drying rack opened up and set flat on the floor worked adequately.

Photo: Judy Wolff
A drying rack serving as a make-shift obstacle

I set up an obstacle course of broom handles, pool noodles, and driveway markers for Tucker to step over.

For figure-8s indoors, a few chairs and food containers served as anchors. Outside, we walked in figure-8 patterns around trees in the front yard.

I updated the table that I used to chart his daily exercise. (During Tucker's rehabilitation, I updated this chart five times.)

Tucker's Therapy

What to Do	Frequency	Reps/Duration	When to Do	Comment	Last Done
Massage & PROM	Daily		After outside walk	Hydrate before and after	
Stretch	2x per day	15-30 seconds	After walk or heat pack		
Stretch toe flexors	6x per day	3 reps, at least 1 minute each	After walk		
Walk	5x per day	5-10-15 min.		Vary surfaces.	
Sit-Stand				Boot on Left rear foot.	
Circles					
Cavaletti rails					
Figure 8					
Weaves					
Weight shifting	2-3x per day	5-10 reps	Mealtime		
Downward compression	2-3x per day	5-10 reps	Mealtime		
Check foot	Regularly			Abrasions, wearing of nail	
Apply Show Foot	2x week				

Other things to do throughout the day:

- Massage or rub his leg, toes to hip
- Tickle and spread his toes
- Tap up and down his leg
- Play footsie

Updated version of daily exercise log

Tucker had a tendency to stick his leg out as a crutch, so that was one thing to watch and correct.

Photo: Judy Wolff

Tucker using his leg as a crutch

Another concern was knuckling, because Tucker wasn't lifting his knee high enough. To practice lifting his lower leg, we walked on sidewalks with curbs, stepping down and then stepping up.

I needed to watch that Tucker sat straight so he would be in a good position to transition to standing.

For the first six months after the FCE, progress did not follow a straight linear path. We'd have good days and some not-so-good days. Tucker would show some improvement, then slow down. We just played it by ear, judging how long to spend on physical therapy exercises and how far and how fast to walk by Tucker's energy and strength at the time. Charlie made it clear that if we did too much too soon, Tucker could have a relapse, so slow and steady was a better course than pushing him.

Exactly six weeks after the FCE, on July 15, Tucker saw Dr. Silver for another neurological exam. She gave us permission to use a crate and let Tucker climb stairs. Tucker also got the green light to play with other dogs, as long as he didn't jump and was not jumped on. Wrestling was also taboo, but that wasn't one of his sports anyway. (He hated wearing the singlet.)

Dr. Silver said that Tucker would probably always be a "little gimpy" on that leg and he would probably plateau at some point. She didn't think he would get to 100%, but he could continue to progress for six months.

She also removed another restriction: swimming. What great news for a Lab, especially mid-summer. Swimming was permitted only if Tucker didn't have to walk far to the water. (That immediately ruled out one of our favorite clean-water swimming sites.) Also, I would have to walk him into the water before throwing a retrieve toy; he should not be bounding in and out of the water.

Tucker's progress was sufficient that he would not need any more neurological visits.

Nearing the end of July, Tucker was able to walk one of our previously regular walking routes around the neighborhood. Before his FCE, this walk took just five minutes, and was a good warm-up or cool-down from a longer walk. That short walk took seventeen minutes now, and Tucker needed a long nap afterwards. We needed to build more stamina, that's all.

My friend Mary and I took Tucker swimming at a lake in a neighboring town. Dogs are not permitted on the people beach, but are tolerated at the boat launch adjacent to the beach. I parked six feet from the water, and, as I helped Tucker out of the car, a man walked toward us. He pulled out his cell phone. I thought he was going to call the police. Mary and I started to explain how Tucker was disabled and needed to swim for therapy, and that we thought dogs were permitted here. Then he held up his phone to show me the display—a photo of his own Labrador Retriever.

Tucker had a fabulous time in the water. I would toss a floating toy we called "the cigar," he'd swim out to retrieve it, well, you know the game. After five minutes, I could see his left hind leg was shaking as he stood, so we called it a day.

The lake swimming was fun for Tucker, but frustrating for me because I couldn't see how much his leg was actually moving underwater.

Photo: Judy Wolff
**Tucker at the lake with his "cigar" retrieve toy.
(He is not wearing a boot because he is on soft sand.)**

Around this time, Kathy Fardy emailed me to ask if Tucker was permitted to swim yet. She said one of her clients, Kristen Dineen Sullivan, would let Tucker swim in her gunite pool!

Kristen later emailed me herself with this generous invitation.

That pool was a godsend. Tucker swam in Kristen's pool several times that summer, gradually building strength.

I timed his sessions, starting with five minutes, and gradually increased his swim time.

He got practice going up and down stairs at the pool's edge. (I would call him out of the pool for a bit of hot dog, to give him some "reps" of climbing stairs.)

I was able to watch his movements underwater, something that I couldn't do at the lake, and, whenever he stopped moving his left leg, the swimming session ended for the day.

Photo: Mary Hogan
Tucker swimming in Kristen's pool.
His left hind leg is dragging: time to stop for today!

Tucker made good progress throughout the month of July.

By the end of the month, I was told that we didn't need to schedule any more outpatient physical therapy sessions, but he wouldn't be officially discharged for another six weeks.

If he needed physical therapy again before those six weeks were up, he could come back without having to undergo another full (expensive) re-evaluation.

Of course we got some new exercises to do at home: more walking, incline/decline walking, "dancing," and climbing and descending short flights of stairs.

I was told that we should walk more and swim more.

We were permitted to play tug (within certain parameters to protect his back), and he could use his skateboard, which would give him practice walking on just the hind legs.

Our goals were now to build strength and endurance, eventually to walk thirty minutes at a pop. We would also work to improve function, coordination, and balance.

We walked out of the hospital. Going downstairs, Tucker walked normally, alternated legs, and bore weight on his left hind leg. I'm sure that was his way of saying, "I'm b*aaaaaaaaaaaaa*ck!"

And we didn't need to return to physical therapy.

For the rest of the summer, we continued our walks, swims, and physical therapy exercises, including stair climbing.

On September 3, we celebrated Tucker's 9th birthday with a cupcake. Tucker and I were still sleeping on the air mattress in the living room.

Then, one September evening, I headed upstairs to brush my teeth. Tucker got up from the bed in the living room, zoomed through the kitchen and dining room, squeezed past the partially open baby gate blocking the stairs, and proceeded to walk upstairs. I helped him the rest of the way. A huge milestone: on September 8, we both slept in our own beds for the first time since May 31.

October brought a few more milestones. One morning, early in the month, Tucker took a few steps backwards, and didn't land on his butt.

We phased out acupuncture at the end of October, and continued working on building Tucker's strength and stamina on our own.

The best October milestone came October 6, four months after his FCE. Tucker had the kind of day that belongs in a dog's diary.

Dear Diary,

This morning I chased a squirrel all the way across the backyard. Then in the afternoon, I chased a bunny across the yard. What fun! I might've caught them, too, if I hadn't slipped.

Backyard critters: 2. Tucker: 0.

Life was returning to normalcy.

7

AND LIFE GOES ON

I write this nearly two years after Tucker's FCE. Tucker is now ten years old.

If I had to quantify his recovery, I'd say Tucker is 90-95% normal, pretty much what Dr. Silver had said would be the best recovery we could expect.

With the perspective of time, I can see that the most trying days were the first month, when we didn't know if he would ever walk again. The first days, especially those first two weeks, were grueling, just adjusting to the changes in routine and the physical demands of holding up the back end of a 75-lb dog for many, many minutes at a time. After that first month, life was mostly normal, or we had so adapted to a new normal that it was no longer an adventure.

Our last instructions from the physical therapist were to keep doing what we were doing and to give him time; never give up.

On a typical day, we walk twice, a combined distance of about a mile or mile and a half. We walk a continuous mile several times a week, in less than thirty minutes (including sniffing and potty breaks).

Before his FCE, we walked a mile or more twice daily. Our shorter walks are .4 miles or .7 miles, both convenient loops in our neighborhood, where Tucker can greet his human and doggy friends. He is able to walk for thirty minutes at a time, what had been our long-term goal.

Tucker can run for short distances, with a gait akin to a bunny hop, and he can outrun me. (But so can a pineapple.) Tucker's stride is periodically interrupted by slip-sliding. He doesn't care; he gets up and keeps going. He picks up his leg over obstacles, except when he's tired, when he drags it more. (Similar to how my shifting deteriorates when I'm too tired to drive.)

The length and pace of our walks depend on how Tucker is feeling and the weather. A ten-year-old dog can occasionally skip a walk without going nuts.

Last March, nine months after his FCE, I scheduled Tucker to participate in a supervised playgroup. He had not played with dogs since before his injury. He had ample opportunity to meet other neighborhood dogs on walks, but that's not the same.

I wanted his first experience to be a safe one, in a controlled environment. Kathy Fardy's playgroup would be perfect, because the dogs have all been "approved." Kathy, a certified pet dog trainer, has trained (or is training) each of the dogs, and she knows their idiosyncracies. Plus, the owners are all present and supervising the dogs. Kathy gives a running commentary on what each dog is doing, pointing out which behaviors are acceptable and which aren't. She teaches the dog parents how to tell when a dog is uncomfortable, acting like a bully, or giving another dog a deserved correction. She also steps in when a dog shows signs of arousal before it escalates.

Tucker enjoys Kathy's playgroups and I knew he would be able to participate safely.

At first, he alternated between clinging to me and checking out the bushes. Then he ventured to see which people would give him treats. (They all did.) Next, he hung out with the smaller dogs, sniffing and marking all corners of the yard. Eventually, he got the courage to offer a play-bow to an old black Lab, who was the spitting image of Sheena. Finally, he joined in briefly with the big dogs. A successful outing! Time to go home and nap.

Tucker of course swims as often as we can manage, when the water temperature is warm enough at the lake, or when Kristen's pool is available. He is a strong swimmer and loves being in the water.

Photo: Judy Wolff

Loving the water

One day at the lake last summer, he swam past his retrieve toy and kept going, to the amusement of everyone at the beach, to fetch the granddaddy of all retrieve items, a big orange "ball" a few yards ahead. The "ball" was the buoy. Tucker tugged at the buoy, trying to loosen it from the ropes. The incident stopped being funny when his body position went from horizontal to vertical, and it became evident he had stopped trying to retrieve the buoy, but was holding on to stay afloat. A lifeguard swam out to help him. One of Tucker's legs had become entangled in the rope. Since then, Tucker wears a doggy life jacket at the lake. It doesn't impede his swimming stroke, and if he were ever to get entangled again, it would keep him afloat until help arrived.

Throughout Tucker's rehabilitation, I updated the checklist that I used to keep track of his exercises. After a few months, instead of a daily checklist, I kept a weekly record.

Tucker's Therapy

Date:

What to Do	Frequency	Reps/Duration	Mon.	Tue.	Wed.	Thurs.	Fri.	Sat.	Sun.
Stretch toe flexors	1-2x per day	3 reps, at least 1 minute each							
Walk Boot on Left rear foot.	daily	Build up to 30 min.							
Sit-Stand Don't fully sit or stand.	2-3x per day	5-10							
Circles/Fig 8									
Cavaletti rails									
SLOW									
Incline/decline See instructions.									
Tug									
Stairs									
Check foot	Regularly								

The weekly log to track Tucker's walks and exercises

Tucker's foot still knuckles, just enough that he wears his booty outside. Given that the knuckling hasn't improved in more than a year, he probably will always be booted. I no longer need to keep an eye on his booty to make sure it hasn't fallen off. The custom boots stay on, and my ear is now trained to recognize the swoosh-clonk-swoosh-clonk sound of his foot hitting and dragging along the pavement.

Photo: Mary Hogan
Tucker wearing his custom red "boo-tay"

Photo: Mary Hogan
A closer look at the "boo-tay"

Every day someone asks, "What happened to your dog's foot?" Just as business people have a one-minute elevator speech, I have a brief reply, "The boot protects his nails and paw because he drags the foot, as a result of a stroke."

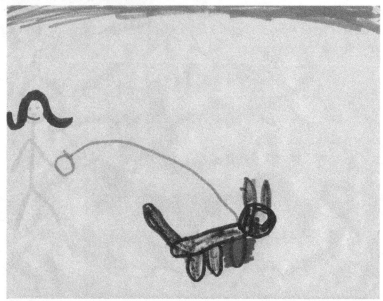

Illustration: Elish Flynn

**My favorite rendition of Tucker wearing his red boot.
Drawn by six-year-old (at the time) neighbor, Elish Flynn.
I'm the skinny person (I wish!) holding the leash.**

Tucker still uses a ramp to go from the deck to the backyard. He is able to maneuver the three steps, but there's a potential he'll slip. I'd rather be cautious than risk his acquiring a fear of stairs. As I said, he's somewhat neurotic. Some days he finds the ramp baffling and stands at the bottom and barks, waiting for me to cheerlead him up. Other days he fearlessly dashes up and down (often jumping off halfway down, giving mom conniption fits).

When Tucker goes up a flight of stairs, I trail as a spotter, to provide a little boost when needed. If he were to slip...no, I'm not finishing this sentence.

Descending a staircase, he wears his seatbelt harness. I hold the handle just to "brake" his speed. He doesn't need support. Sometimes he moves the leg while going downstairs, and sometimes he drags it. Whatever is the fastest way downstairs (where the food is).

Photo: Judy Wolff
Tucker going downstairs in his harness, with his left hind leg trailing

Slippery floors pose a challenge. Hardwood, tile, and wet surfaces are slippery and scary. Mostly scary; much of the problem is in his head. Tucker has no problem when walking slowly, or when he doesn't think about the floors, such as when he's chasing after a toy. However, since he is afraid to slip, he scampers, increasing the likelihood that he will slip.

I've strategically positioned area rugs on the hardwood floors to provide a continuous footpath with traction.

A few months ago, we replaced the ceramic tile floor in the kitchen with vinyl for better traction—and to get rid of the fur-trapping nonskid mats.

Tucker is still superstitious about certain spots on the floor. For example, instead of walking a straight line from his bed (in the center of the kitchen) to the back door, he'll walk into the dining room and from there to the back door. He has decided that is a safe path; the direct path, for whatever reason (maybe he slipped once?) is dangerous.

Should a guest exit the bathroom and leave the door open, there's no chance Tucker would venture inside. At his bravest he will put his front paws on the tiled floor. (Still, I don't recommend a spinal injury as a way of keeping your dog away from the toilet paper roll.)

For nearly a year, Tucker would fall backwards if he tried to step backwards. He now has enough leg strength that he can walk backwards for several steps. So, if he gets wedged between the sofa and coffee table (where odds are good he'll find crumbs), he can back out of the space on his own, and he doesn't need someone to move the table.

Falls where his legs splay like Bambi on the ice occur several times a week: running in the yard, walking in the snow, or going too fast in the kitchen. Mom no longer panics at these. Tucker gets up (sometimes with assistance), and goes about his doggly ways.

His balance is actually quite good. He makes two concessions: he rarely lifts a leg, but instead shifts his hips forward when he urinates (no, he doesn't wet his feet). He often walks with his tail up in the pre-poop position, presumably as counterbalance.

Photo: Judy Wolff

Tail-up position for balance

Photo: Judy Wolff

Tail-up position for balance.
Tucker, dressed as a gym rat on Halloween, is wearing a muscle shirt and bandana and carrying a dumbbell.

Tucker fatigues easily, which shows up as dragging his leg or leg tremors. These are signs to curtail the walk, or to skip a walk. After a slow one-mile walk on leash, Tucker will sleep for hours.

Since I see him all the time, I don't notice much change. But friends and neighbors who see him less frequently claim he shows continued improvement.

Tucker's spirits are good, and his body is pain-free. He's always up for a good session of tug, fetch, or cuddling. He doesn't seem to notice or care that he has physical limitations. For a ten-year-old dog, he is doing more than OK.

In terms of trust and bonding, he understands that I will keep the world safe for him and protect him, so he doesn't need to display defensive postures.

I recently "promoted" him for good behavior, permitting him up on the futon. After all we've shared in the last seven years, he's earned the privilege.

Was this experience a blessing in disguise, a spiritual awakening, a wonderful opportunity to build trust and confidence in my dog, something to be grateful for? No, it was a frightening, exhausting, stressful experience. It was challenging, both physically and emotionally. I would rather not have gone through this experience. But Tucker and I didn't have a choice.

And we got through it, mostly unscathed.

If I had to go through the rehab again, would I? Yes, simply because my dog can walk.

Several times a day I get a spine-tingling thrill just by calling, "Tucker, come!" and watching my handsome, happy, and healthy Lab joyfully bound across the yard, up the ramp, and into the house. His gait may not be perfect, and he may be dragging his foot, but it's poetry in motion.

IF AN FCE STRIKES YOUR DOG

If an FCE strikes your dog, first, my wishes for the best possible outcome.

Here are some tips that might help you manage day-to-day.

Rehab exercises and progression

I am a pet owner. I am supremely *not* qualified to give any advice on an exercise program for your dog.

Consult those who have the appropriate training and experience: veterinarians and canine physical therapists. Don't ask your friends, dog trainer, or the pet sitter.

The appropriate exercises depend on the nature and severity of your individual dog's trauma, especially any injury to the spinal column. Don't mess with spinal injuries.

Please be aware that the rehabilitation program I followed with Tucker might not work for your dog. You can do everything right but your dog still might not respond. Each dog's recovery depends on the specifics of his injury. We were lucky, and I was able to exploit that luck.

Gear

Show Foot™

Spray Show Foot™ on the bottom of your dog's paws to improve traction. The product is sold through catalogs and on websites for show dogs and agility. For best results, spray it on when the dog is lying down after exercise, and is too tired to walk around. Then wait at least eight minutes for it to fully dry before letting the dog stand.

Slings

The Bottom's-Up Leash™ looked nice and worked fine for short periods, but it took time to put on, a factor when your dog has to go out *now*. It was difficult to hold for long periods, but is probably comfortable for short spells.

The bandage type of sling was not the prettiest, but it was the easiest to put on quickly and was machine washable.

Get several slings so you always have a clean one.

These are also lightweight and easy to shove in a pocket or over a shoulder, so you can keep both hands free.

Keep one in the car for convenience.

Boots

The off-the-rack boots slip off. It is hard to get a good fit because dog shoe sizes are not standardized.

Custom boots are more costly but they stay on. They have heavy-duty material on the bottom and over the toes. They're also machine-washable, an important feature when the dog urinates and then drags his foot through the puddle.

My experience is that the boots wear out in four to six weeks, depending on use and terrain. I usually buy two pairs at a time. (I could extend their life by dipping them in Plasti-Dip®, but I choose not to.)

Harness

The harness we use (the Roadie™) is the one I bought to secure Tucker in the car. The strap goes across his chest and not around his neck.

Besides using the harness in the car, I use it to assist Tucker when he goes downstairs.

Wherever Tucker goes, the harness goes, too.

Ramps

A wooden ramp is sturdier, steadier, and requires less training than a plastic ramp (which tends to have some bounce).

If you build one yourself, make it long enough so that its incline isn't steep.

If you can make the ramp wide (about thirty inches), it will be easier for you and your dog to walk together side-by-side.

Nonskid material for ramp and stairs

A wooden ramp gets slick when wet.

You can buy nonskid tape for traction. Be aware that the tape lasts about a season in severe weather (such as New England) and then wears off.

You can paint the ramp with nonskid paint (paint with sand mixed in), but a dog's nails, even with weekly trimming, will scratch off the paint. The paint also provides no useful traction in snow and ice.

We eventually installed aluminum treads on the ramp and the stairs. These were pricy but held up well through the winter and will probably outlast both the ramp and the stairs.

Stairs

- Install baby gates to prevent unsupervised use if your dog has difficulty navigating stairs.
- Use a sling to help your dog go up.
- Use a harness or sling to brace your dog when you go down.
- Keep a phone in your pocket in case you fall and need to call for help.

If you "camp out" downstairs with your dog

- Block him in so he can't crawl away and get stuck somewhere.
- Have a phone, lamp, and/or flashlight within reach. I used a battery-operated camp lamp.
- Keep your dog's sling nearby. (You can see Tucker's sling on the floor in some of the photos of our "campsite" in the living room.)
- In case you need help from others at home in the middle of the night, get an inexpensive pair of walkie-talkies. They are easier and more effective than shouting to awaken the rest of the household.

Crating

- If a crate isn't allowed, consider using an x-pen.
- Move or block any furniture your dog might attempt to climb.
- Brace the x-pen so it doesn't topple over.
- Move out of reach anything you do not want your dog eating or chewing.

- Leave a safe toy (such as a Kong® toy stuffed with treats) with your dog to keep him busy when alone.

- Put his water dish within your dog's reach. Put something absorbent underneath the water dish, in case it is tipped over.

- Put the x-pen far enough from windows and doors that your dog won't be tempted to stand up to see anyone coming.

- Mask outside sounds (such as cars passing on the street) with a radio if your dog is likely to react to the sounds. Your dog may be more stressed than usual by his immobility.

- If your dog shows anxiety, try using one of the pheromone products, such as Comfort Zone®.

Incontinence

- Place absorbent material, such as towels on the floor. A lightweight, absorbent, machine-washable ground cover called the Neat Sheet (made by Kimberly-Clark and sold in the summer at some pharmacy chains) is useful for covering a large area.

- Use bladder control products made for humans or for canines (diapers for females in heat, belly bands for incontinent males). Minipads and sanitary napkins might be insufficient to catch the output of a full bladder. Products made for incontinent adults or toddlers are more absorbent. For the best recommendation on specific products (brand and style), consult an expert: the mother of a toddler who needs overnight protection.

- Stock up on enzymatic clean up products, the kind that eliminate odors instead of masking them. Even better, readily available, and less expensive is white vinegar.

- Keep your dog clean and dry to avoid "diaper rash."

- Be aware that you may need to express your dog's bladder. Your veterinarian will let you know if you need to do so, and, if so, how to do it. I did not have to express Tucker's bladder.

APPENDIX A

Chronology

The following chronology is a reproduction of my notes and excerpts from my emails throughout Tucker's rehabilitation, thus the shorthand writing style.

June 1: Active, healthy eight-year-old dog goes down with a yelp and can't get up.

June 2: X-rays and examination at our veterinarian led to a referral to Massachusetts Veterinary Referral Hospital in Woburn, where he had additional tests. Left hind leg is paralyzed. Unable to fully wag tail.

June 3: Prepare the house for Tucker's return. The right hind leg is strong enough for him to stand on so he can walk assisted with a sling.

June 4: Discharged from hospital, starts physical therapy (outpatient) and home care. Physical therapy (at hospital, as outpatient) includes stretches, underwater treatmill, Cavaletti rails, balance/wobble board.

Tucker and I are sleeping together in the living room on an air mattress.

June 5: Licks foot, pins-and-needles sensation?

June 6: Physical therapist feels some muscle tone in inner thigh while walking on underwater treadmill, some superficial pain.

June 7: Full tail wag! Leg twitches while he sleeps (it's very exciting to see *any* movement).

June 10: Start acupuncture immediately after physical therapy session. Pins-and-needles must be bothering him. While I slept, he chewed his foot and developed a hot spot.

June 11-14: Occasional leg twitches, involuntary reflex movement of leg. Twitched when I sprayed Show Foot™.

June 15: Started to "click/treat" for involuntary pulling of leg and correct foot position; this pulling was exciting because it was forceful.

June 16: Partial weight-bearing but no voluntary control of leg. Still needs sling support to walk.

June 17: Physical therapist notes that he is moving hip and walking like Chester from *Gunsmoke* on underwater treadmill. Most movement is still reflex.

June 18: In morning, still needed a lot of support with sling. By afternoon, neurologist observes progress in last two weeks (actually, since yesterday, but she hadn't seen him for two weeks), says OK to let him stand without a sling on good surfaces as actually he took some steps!!!

June 19: Occasionally straightens foot into correct position, walking a little (as far as next door).

June 20-21: His personality is back! He's feisty, feeling good, and wants to go. Got away from dog walker, while she was putting his boot back on him. He went to visit a neighbor across street to get a cookie. First hands-on Reiki session.

June 21: Another hands-on Reiki session. During a leg extension stretch, he uncurled his foot.

June 22: Using leg more, sometimes stands without knuckling. Sometimes fixes knuckling on his own.

June 23: Starting to eliminate on cue outside, but he still hasn't asked to go out since FCE. Last accident inside was June 16 so has some bladder/bowel control.

June 24: Physical therapist observes him walking in for treatment and says, "Wow!" Notes "significant" progress in a week.

For first time on Cavaletti rails the leg doesn't drag—he picks up leg for each rail and places down, positioning foot correctly (without knuckling).

Still extends left leg a lot for support, but is able to move the entire leg, for the first time.

For first time shows "conscious proprioception" (awareness of where his leg and foot are in space). He is positioning his foot, without knuckling, about a third of the time.

June 25: Walked a few houses down the street. Butt-tucked in backyard. At physical therapy, got out of car and started to pee. I asked him to wait, he stopped the flow, and took him to grass. He can control the stream!

June 26: Walked to end of the street (two houses) in one direction and back, plus another two houses. Showing fatigue afterwards, but gait is improved.

June 27: Walking with all four legs. Gait is mostly normal (alternating legs), some knuckling but less.

He appears to have control of bladder and bowels but does not have the early warning system that tells him in advance when he needs to go, so we take him out every couple of hours. He has had a few accidents in the house the last few weeks because by the time he realizes he needs to go, he's already going.

When he is fatigued, he drags and swings the leg under his body and across other leg.

June 30: Spent day at doggy daycare (dog walker on vacation). Visited Dr. Brewer, first time she saw him since FCE.

July 1: One month since FCE.

July 2: Walked our usual short walk (.4 mile) without dragging his leg.

July 7: Dog walker returns from one-week vacation and notices substantial improvement.

July 15: Walk around neighborhood .7 miles. Too much; he's fatigued and weaker next day, so we ratchet back.

July 17: Swim at Long Lake.

July 24: Still driving twice a week for physical therapy and acupuncture, doing physical therapy exercises at home several times a day.

I'm getting out 1-1.5 hours a day, with the dog walker coming in for a half hour at the midway point.

Tucker can be crated, but I won't leave him more than an hour or so at a time. I've been taking him outside every hour or two.

He still can't go up and down stairs. He can walk around the block, a walk that used to take five minutes now takes seventeen minutes. He sometimes drags his leg and his foot. His foot is no longer totally curled up and he can position it correctly.

End of July: Tucker discharged from physical therapy, will continue acupuncture weekly. Goal is to build up stamina to walk thirty minutes.

August: Swimming as often as possible, either at Long Lake or in Kristen's swimming pool. Walking on days he doesn't swim. Walking or swimming, working in structured PT exercises when possible (weather-space-energy permitting).

September 3: Tucker turns 9 years old.

September 8: Tucker and I sleep in our own beds!

October 3: Took a few steps backwards without falling back. (This promising sign turned out to be a fluke. It took nearly a year of rehab before Tucker could step backwards with any consistency.)

October 6: Chased a squirrel across the yard, later chased a bunny.

October: Phased out acupuncture at end of month.

November 12: Tucker is coming along, some good days, some tough days. We typically walk around the block, .4 miles, twice a day.

He had a great annual physical last week, and, for a nine-year-old, is doing OK. He can now squat to poop and hold the position, a sign of improved strength.

Late November: Develops phobia about going up three steps from backyard to deck (which he has been doing without incident since late June). Barks and waits for help. It is totally in his head, because he can do it when I stand near him, without giving him any assistance.

Have one acupuncture session to see if it helps; it doesn't.

Early December: Still phobic about coming in from backyard, so, with impending snowstorm, we move ramp from driveway to backyard. Now Tucker doesn't recognize the ramp, and barks at foot of ramp for help going up.

He is OK on days the ramp is covered with snow, but when it is clear, he can't figure out how to get on it. Approaches from the side, barks, then goes to other side, barks. I train him just like it is the dog walk, with treats set up at intervals. He goes up, takes the first treat, then turns around and starts over.

He sometimes backs up seven or eight times until he makes an approach he likes and then dashes up ramp.

End December: The stairs going up from the driveway were slippery one day and he slid back from the bottom step. He didn't get hurt but got scared and is now afraid to go up those steps. A cookie tossed on deck and lots of cheerleading will eventually do the trick, but he goes up two steps at a time, and I stand behind him to spot.

January 2009: Not seeing many changes physically. Still walking twice a day. Some days he still fatigues enough that leg trembles.

Gets in and out of car fine.

Still needs a spotter to go upstairs and harness to hold him back going down long staircase. He's fine going down short flights (three or four steps) without help.

Still have rubber backed mats all over house. He is jittery about walking on a tiled floor. He usually goes through the dining room to the living room to avoid a small gap in the mats, though I am working on teaching him "slow" so that he doesn't skitter, which is when he slips.

More work to go in learning how to use the ramp and to go slow on slippery surfaces.

June 2009: One year and six days after FCE, he walked a mile. Walked that route again the following week, in only twenty-eight minutes. Continue to walk a mile several times a week.

Appendix B

RESOURCES

Your comments

If you would like to send the author or Tucker a message, email: tucker.fce@gmail.com.

Videos of Tucker

Visit Tucker's channel on YouTube to see videos of him taken an hour after his FCE and six weeks later.

There are also recent videos of him walking, running, and performing some of his favorite tricks.

www.youtube.com/tuckerfce

The video about Labrador Retriever Rescue, Inc., where Tucker can be seen running in the yard with children, is on Labrador Retriever Rescue's YouTube channel:

www.youtube.com/labrescuevideo

Canine acupuncture

For information about acupuncture, or to find a veterinarian licensed to practice acupuncture:

The International Veterinary Acupuncture Society:

www.ivas.org

The American Academy of Veterinary Acupuncture:

www.aava.org

CGC

The Canine Good Citizen is a certification program for dogs that have good manners in the house and in public.

http://www.akc.org/events/cgc/index.cfm

Clicker training

The best place to start learning about clicker training is Karen Pryor's website:

www.clickertraining.com

Freecycle

Freecycle is a grassroots network of local groups promoting the reuse of goods, rather than discarding more stuff in landfills. You join a local email list and post what items you have to give away, or what you need. Membership and all goods given or received are free.

www.freecycle.org

Labrador Retriever Rescue

Labrador Retriever Rescue, Inc. is a 501(c)3 nonprofit, volunteer organization dedicated to placing purebred Labrador Retrievers in suitable, loving homes. Labs are accepted from, and placed in, the following states *only*: Maine, Massachusetts, New Hampshire, Rhode Island, and Vermont. Labrador Retriever Rescue, Inc. was incorporated in 1988 and is the original rescue organization for Labrador Retrievers in New England.

www.labrescue.com   24-hour hotline: 978-356-2982

Information on other rescue organizations serving this breed is available on the parent site of the Labrador Retriever Club: www.thelabradorclub.com.

Reiki

For everything you wanted to know about Reiki:

www.reiki.org

Websites with useful information and links

The following sites, besides selling mobility aids (such as wheels) for pets, have helpful articles:

www.handicappedpet.net

www.eddieswheels.com

Businesses and products mentioned in this book

I am providing information about products and businesses I have used as a convenience to you. I am not responsible for these products, services, or information. Use the information at your own discretion and risk.

Businesses & professional practices

Dog's Time (Kathy Fardy)
P.O. Box 1133, Billerica, Massachusetts 01821
www.dogstime.com

Gemini Dogs
53-B Ayer Road, Littleton, Massachusetts 01460
www.geminidogs.com

Hoof, Paw & Claw (Aileen D'Angelo)
www.reikiforcritters.com

The Lyman Center (Gale Lyman)
58 Macy Street, Amesbury MA 01913
www.lymancenter.com

Massachusetts Veterinary Referral Hospital
20 Cabot Road, Woburn MA 01801
www.InTownMassVet.com

Products

Bottom's Up Leash™ Harness

A padded sling for mobility assistance.

www.bottomsupleash.com

Comfort Zone® Diffuser

A drug-free stress-reliever for dogs, using pheromones.

www.petcomfortzone.com

Handi-Ramp™ Stair Treads

Aluminum treads to prevent slipping on steps and ramp.

www.handiramp.com

Kong®

A toy that you can stuff with food to keep your dog busy.

www.kongcompany.com

Roadie™ Seatbelt Harness

The harness I use for car rides and descending stairways.
www.ruffrider.com
www.AnimalWorldNetwork.com

Show Foot™ Anti-Slip Spray

A spray to aid traction, made by Bio-Groom.
http://www.biogroom.com/index.htm

Tammy and Teddy's Booties

Tucker's custom boots are made by Tammy and Teddy's.
www.tammyandteddys.com

Ordering Information

Web orders:

www.lulu.com/jftm

For information on wholesale and bulk pricing:

Email: pubs-sales@jftm.biz

Copies of this book with your clinic's name printed on the cover ("Compliments of *Your Animal Hospital*") are available for large orders. For information on special orders:

Email: info@jftm.biz

Publisher information: www.jftm.biz

CPSIA information can be obtained
at www.ICGtesting.com
Printed in the USA
LVHW091347080521
686873LV00005B/208